M000104815

SICKLE AND CRESCENT:
THE COMMUNIST REVOLT OF 1926
IN BANTEN

Michael C. Williams

SICKLE AND CRESCENT: THE COMMUNIST REVOLT OF 1926 IN BANTEN

EQUINOX
PUBLISHING
JAKARTA KUALA LUMPUR

Equinox Publishing (Asia) Pte Ltd
No 3. Shenton Way
#10-05 Shenton House
Singapore 068805

www.EquinoxPublishing.com

Sickle And Crescent:
The Communist Revolt of 1926 in Banten
by Michael C. Williams

ISBN 978-602-8397-53-7

First Equinox Edition 2010

Copyright © 1982 by Cornell Southeast Asia
Program Publications; renewed 2010.
This is a reprint edition authorized by the original publisher,
Cornell Southeast Asia Program Publications.

Printed in the United States

1 3 5 7 9 10 8 6 4 2

All rights reserved. No part of this publication may be reproduced, stored in
a retrieval system, or transmitted in any form or by any means, electronic,
mechanical, photocopying, recording or otherwise without the prior
permission of Equinox Publishing.

TABLE OF CONTENTS

CHAPTER ONE
BACKGROUND TO THE REVOLT*

"Alongside the crescent, the star of the Soviets will be the great battle emblem…"

Tan Malaka[1]

"Just as unclean cloth must be washed with soap, so an impure world must be cleansed by blood."

Haji Achmad Chatib[2]

Twice in this century the people of Banten have risen in revolt against those they considered to be their oppressors. On both occasions the leadership of the revolts was largely religious and yet at the same time announced to all that it was Communist. The revolutionary leadership successfully portrayed their ideology as both past and future. In 1926 and again in 1945, revolt was to be the harbinger of freedom from colonial rule and the dawn of a new era of social justice and prosperity. These are familiar themes of Communist-inspired revolt, but the Bantenese revolutionaries also delved deep into their past history to proclaim that the advent of Communist revolt would also lead to the restoration of the Sultanate of Banten.

The Banten region illustrates strikingly that the movement from "archaic" to modern forms of political protest is not lineal but dialectical. As Geertz has perceptively remarked, "there is in such matters no simple

*   The author wishes to express his appreciation to Ruth T. McVey for her comments on this text.
1   Tan Malaka, "De Islam en het Bolsjewisme," *De Tribune*, September 21, 1922, cited in Ruth T. McVey, *The Rise of Indonesian Communism* (Ithaca: Cornell University Press, 1965), p. 161.
2   Statement to the Police of Diarman of Caringin, October 6, 1926, Mailr 637x/ 1927, Vb April 13, 1928 06.

progression from 'traditional' to 'modern,' but a twisting, spasmodic, unmethodical movement which turns as often toward repossessing the emotions of the past as disowning them."[3] This dialectical connection between future, present, and past was evident not only in the ideology of the two main revolts, but also in the social composition of the revolutionary leadership. In both uprisings descendants of the former Sultans of Banten, called *tubagus*, and others holding noble titles they had borne from old, played a prominent role. Indeed one of the very first actions of the Indonesian Communist Party (PKI) branch in 1925 was to demand compensation and pensions for all who bore the title tubagus from a sultanate abolished nearly a century before. They rubbed shoulders in the revolutionary leadership with other traditional leaders of peasant revolt, such as the Islamic teachers, the *ulama*, and the local men of violence, the *jawara*, but also with more "modern" revolutionaries such as artisans, printers, journalists, and trade unionists. In short, the uncompromising insistence on modernity that was to be a hallmark of the PKI after 1951 was certainly not a prominent feature of the movement in the 1920s or in 1945. The PKI of the 1950s and 1960s made a rejection of the past a key part of its revolutionary image. This was not the case in an earlier era.[4]

Islamic communism is seemingly a paradox. This is especially the case when one considers that probably no religion has proved more resistant to the ideology of communism than Islam. One common feature of both the Soviet Union and the People's Republic of China today is the persistence of strong Islamic minorities and traditions despite decades of socialist rule. Yet at the same time we have to account for the fact that in certain historical periods and in certain countries a social movement has flourished which can aptly be called "Islamic Communism." This was

---

3   Clifford Geertz, "Afterword: The Politics of Meaning," in *Culture and Politics in Indonesia*, ed. Claire Holt et al. (Ithaca: Cornell University Press, 1972), p. 328.

4   The PKP's stress on the theme of modernity in the 1950s and 1960s has been pointed out by Ruth McVey in "Enchantment of the Revolution," in *Perceptions of the Past*, ed. David Marr and Anthony Reid (Singapore: Heineman, 1980), pp. 340-58. Informants in Banten, particularly those who had been active in the PKI in 1925-26, often drew a distinction between the Communist Party of that period and the post-1951 PKI led by D. N. Aidit. The differences that informants pointed out related not only to the attitude Communists should adopt towards Islam, but also that the PKI of the 1920s was far more tolerant of local traditions, hierarchies, and customs than its latter-day counterpart.

palpably the case in Indonesia in the 1920s and was also true of several of the local Communist movements that appeared in the aftermath of the Japanese collapse in 1945.

Many early Indonesian Communist leaders, such as Tan Malaka, believed that Islam could be harnessed to the revolutionary cause.[5] Others, such as Haji Misbach[6] and the Bantenese leader, Haji Achmad Chatib, went even further and argued that there was no fundamental incompatibility between Islam and communism. It was, of course, somewhat easier to adopt such a position in a colonized Indonesia than it was in the postcolonial Republic. In the early twentieth century the national bourgeoisie as a social class was extremely weak in Indonesia and, more importantly, foreign rule and capitalism were seen as one and the same thing. Moreover, at least until the 1920s, Islam and Indonesian nationalism were so closely identified as to be almost synonymous.[7]

The spectacular development of the PKI in the 1920s was due in no small measure to the fact that it did not reject Indonesia's Islamic traditions. But, despite this, the party was remarkably slow in developing a base in an area long known for its Islamic orthodoxy and for a history punctuated with uprisings against Dutch colonial rule. As late as March 1925, the retiring Dutch Resident could write: "The population of Banten is extremely devout and staunchly conservative, so that communism will find no scope for development here."[8] The reasons for this are not too difficult to surmise. The economic and social development of Java during the nineteenth century had largely bypassed Banten, leaving it an isolated and neglected region. Together with strong regional traditions and particularities, this made the development of new social and political

---

5   On Tan Malaka's views of the need for an alliance between Communists and revolutionary Islam, see Harry Poeze, *Tan Malaka Levensloop van 1897 tot 1945: Strijder voor Indonesië's Vrijheid* (The Hague: Nijhoff, 1976), pp. 138, 149, 225-26; Petrus Blumberger, *De Communistische Beweging in Nederlandsch-Indië* (Haarlem: Tjeenk Willink, 1928), pp. 65ff.; McVey, Rise, pp. 161-62; Jeanne S. Mintz, "Marxism in Indonesia," in Marxism in Southeast Asia, ed. Frank N. Trager (Palo Alto: Stanford University Press, 1959), p. 179.

6   On Haji Misbach's views see his series of articles, "Islam dan Communisme," *Medan Moeslimin*, 1925-26, written by him in exile in Manokwari, New Guinea (text in my possession). See also McVey, Rise, pp. 172-74; Blumberger, *Communistische Beweging*, pp. 38ff.

7   Deliar Noer, *The Modernist Muslim Movement in Indonesia, 1900-42* (Singapore: Oxford University Press, 1973), p. 7 and passim.

8   *Memorie van Overgave* [hereafter *MvO*] *van den afgetreden Resident van Bantam, J. C. Bedding*, March 24, 1925, p. 68.

forces very difficult. Urbanization, for example, had proceeded at a very slow pace. In 1925 in this region of approximately 950,000 inhabitants only one town, Serang, the residency capital, had a population of more than 10,000.[9] As there were no factories and very few plantations in the area, there was correspondingly almost no working class. The intelligentsia was likewise remarkably small, while the European, Eurasian, and Chinese communities, although they had grown significantly since 1890, were proportionately smaller in Banten than in any other residency of Java. The overwhelming majority of the region's inhabitants were peasant smallholders, although increasingly in the early part of this century very many of them ventured outside the region in search of temporary work. The very poor were to establish themselves permanently in exile.

The peasantry had found social and political leadership traditionally in the ulama or Islamic teachers. This religious elite was profoundly alienated from the colonial order. A small section of the religious leaders had been partially integrated, through their appointment as *penghulu*, the local heads of the mosque functionaries, but generally in Banten these officials did not have the respect of the main body of ulama or *kiyai*, or for that matter of the population as a whole.[10] For the most part the religious leaders remained in sullen isolation from the government, while still enjoying enormous social prestige among the peasantry.

Although Bantenese society was exposed to social and economic change, it was change of a different order from that which affected the rest of Java. The area did not witness the emergence of industry and large-scale commerce as in the island's coastal cities nor for that matter did it see the transformation of agriculture which occurred in Central and East Java with the expansion of plantations and sugar cultivation. Change had occurred with the development of some commodity crops, especially coconuts, and with the demand for migrant labor in Batavia

---

9   *Volkstelling 1930*, I (Landsdrukkerij: Department van Economische Zaken, 1933), pp. 27-28.

10   Harry J. Benda and Ruth T. McVey, eds., *The Communist Uprisings of 1926-1927 in Indonesia: Key Documents* (Ithaca: Cornell Modern Indonesia Project, 1960), p. 38. This collection includes (pp. 19-96) the official report of the government inquiry into the uprising in Banten (referred to hereafter as the "Bantam Report"). On the attitude towards *penghulu*, see also G. F. Pijper, "De Penghulus op Java," in his *Studien over de Geschiedenis van de Islam op Java, 1900-1950* (Leiden: Brill, 1977), pp. 63-96. Pijper makes the point (p. 65) that district and subdistrict penghulu were a phenomenon of recent date, having been established in Banten only in the years 1894-99.

and Sumatra. Peasants took advantage of these opportunities to relieve the new burdens placed on them through population pressure and more efficient tax collection.

During the course of the nineteenth century the colonial state had only slowly encapsulated the Javanese village within its realm. This process was even slower when no overriding economic interests forced it to this course. Only at the beginning of the twentieth century did the colonial government effectively establish its presence in rural Banten, as the region had been little influenced by the major socioeconomic developments of the nineteenth century, such as the Cultivation System or the opening up of the economy to private plantation development after 1870.[11]

It has been widely observed that where the nation state is unable to control and integrate peripheral areas there is room for political middlemen or brokers who are able to bridge the gaps in communication and to exploit them often to retain their own position vis-à-vis the peasantry. In Banten, the religious elite, the ulama, together with the jawara, did perform this role to some extent. Indeed had it not been for countervailing developments, such as the emergence of powerful secular political movements like the Sarekat Islam and the Communist Party, which offered new opportunities to the ulama and the jawara, these groups might have been gradually coopted into the colonial status quo.

The development of the new political forces led, at least for a limited period, to a more adequate articulation of rural discontent, although this was not a clearcut movement towards modern secular politics. Rather it was a process whereby those modern political forces which had arrived on the scene adapted themselves to the concrete realities of the local situation. The normal assumption in analyzing the relationship between the community and the nation state is that the community, the repository of the "Little Tradition," eventually succumbs to the "Great Tradition" of the nation state.[12] The process of political mobilization is said to be typified by the mobilization of local leaders by national leaders and state

---

11 I explore the economic and political background to the revolt in a Ph.D. thesis I am preparing on "The Social History of Banten in the Twentieth Century" at the School of Oriental and African Studies, University of London.

12 Robert Redfield has made the classic statement on this, in his *The Little Community and Peasant Society and Culture* (Chicago: University of Chicago Press, 1965), passim.

institutions.[13] However, it is possible that the process is reversible to some degree, as some writers have suggested.[14] In other words new emerging political forces, in order to gain acceptance in peripheral areas, are often forced to make considerable concessions and adaptations to the "Little Tradition" in order to gain the acceptance of the community.

Certain regions lend themselves particularly well to this resistance to state encroachment and the emergence of new political movements. The latter are only accepted if they are willing to come to terms with the realities of local power. Modern history is replete with examples of regions with a long history of autonomy organizing themselves politically to resist intrusion on their territory, resources, and people. In the Mediterranean,Berbers, Kabyles, and Sicilians pursued this strategy successfully for centuries.[15] Tactical mobility and the skilled use of violence, together with a sparsely populated terrain, assist in this resistance. In Indonesia, the Bantenese were among its most skilled practitioners.

Other significant processes of social change were at work. A growing number of peasants in the Banten region, for example, were beginning to be involved in a wider world outside the village boundaries as migrant workers in Batavia or Sumatra. Even here, however, the process of development was uneven. We find, for example, that among the leaders of the Banten Communist movement exiled to Boven-Digul after 1927 there were a number of peasants who had never been outside their own village, let alone outside Banten. At the same time a new group of social and political actors who had not been present in earlier Bantenese revolts, such as that of 1888,participated in the 1926 revolt. These men were artisans or semi-intellectuals, such as clerks, village schoolteachers, tailors, printers, and mechanics,who had a definite, and sometimes prolonged, experience of life outside Banten, usually in Batavia, as well as some formal education. They provided the necessary link between the PKI as a national political force and the ulama and jawara of Banten. Despite the arrival of this new

---

13 Peter Nettl, *Political Mobilization* (London: Faber & Faber, 1963), passim.
14 Peter Schneider, Jane Schneider, and Edward Hansen, "Modernization and Development: The Role of Regional Elites and Noncorporate Groups in the European Mediterranean," *Comparative Studies in Society and History*, 14 (1972), pp. 328-50.
15 See E. R. Wolf, *Peasant Wars of the Twentieth Century* (London: Faber and Faber, 1969), pp. 238-39, for comments on the Berbers; on Sicily, see especially Anton Blok, *Mafia of a Sicilian Village* (Oxford: Blackwell, 1974), passim.

group on the scene, it was essentially already existing "noncorporate groups"[16] such as the ulama, who were the crucial motor both of the 1926 uprising and of the social revolution of 1945.

But if, as we have argued, the evolution of political and social protest in Banten should not be seen merely as the "Little Tradition" responding to the "Great Tradition," it should be noted that those elements of the community who did not respond to the new imperatives found themselves to some extent isolated and subject to a gradual undermining of their prestige and position. It is the young Haji Achmad Chatib who willingly embraced both the Sarekat Islam and the PKI, who galvanized the Bantenese in both 1926 and 1945, and not his father-in-law the revered ulama, Kiyai Haji Asnawi, who abstained from involvement with the new political forces.

The meeting of the "Little" and "Great" traditions occurred at two levels. On the one hand new political forces such as the Sarekat Islam and the PKI sought local acceptance and, on the other, the effectiveness of the state machinery began to have a growing impact on local society. At the same time economic circumstances were changing. The peasantry were exposed to a new and bewildering environment wherein they had to cope with the individualizing forces of the capitalist market and with the slow and tortuous consolidation of the colonial state. When the available means of redress and of expressing grievances about these changes were strictly limited, the appeal of new forces such as the PKI, which seemed to some almost as powerful as the colonial government, was greatly enhanced.

The Legacy of the Sarekat Islam

In Banten the Sarekat Islam was dominated by the personality of Raden

---

16 Schneider et al. ("Modernization and Development," p. 334) have defined "corporate" and "noncorporate groups" as follows: "A corporate group has legal status, i.e., it is chartered, and controls property which is vested in the group per se. Furthermore, the corporate group has a life of its own; it may well antedate and survive any particular set of members. A non-corporate group is not chartered, although there may well be an ideology, a common mentality, or behavioural grammar which defines the routes of entrance into the group and regulates the conduct of its members. Most important, the assets of a noncorporate group are not vested in the group, per se. They remain the property of its individual members. In short, the noncorporate group may be a coalition, clique or patron-client chain, in which individuals pool resources and skills."

Hasan Djajadiningrat, the younger brother of the Regent of Serang, R. A. A. Achmad Djajadiningrat.[17] Where possible he sought to select carefully the religious leaders joining the organization, preferring those with a moderate outlook such as Raden Mohammed Isa, the chief penghulu of Serang, to the more fiery and uncompromising younger leaders such as Haji Achmad Chatib. However, Hasan's influence was not sufficient to exclude altogether leaders such as Chatib. Where Hasan was more successful in his activity as chairman of the Banten section of the organization, however, was in specifically proscribing jawara and those with a criminal record from the organization.

The death of Hasan Djajadiningrat in 1920 coincided with a toughening Dutch attitude to the Sarekat Islam following the "Afdeling B incident" of the previous year.[18] As elsewhere, this caused the Sarekat Islam to lose much support, particularly in the ranks of those in government employ such as lower ranking *priyayi*, clerks, and schoolteachers. Those branches that were dominated by this group, such as Serang or Rangkasbitung, the main town of Lebak regency, declined rapidly as the Sarekat Islam came under increasing Dutch scrutiny. Elsewhere, as for example in Labuan, Menes, Petir, Cadasari, and Cilegon, the organization continued to

---

17 Hasan Djajadiningrat, born in 1883, was the third son of Raden Tumenggung Djajadiningrat, Regent of Serang (1893-99) and younger brother of R. A. A. Achmad Djajadiningrat, Regent of Serang (1899-1924). Like his elder brother, Hasan enjoyed a Dutch education in Batavia. He was a fellow pupil and close friend of Edward Douwes Dekker, the founder of the Indische Party. Hasan Djajadiningrat was vice-president of the Banten branch of this party until it was declared illegal in 1913. Later he became chairman of the Banten branch of the Sarekat Islam. In August 1914 he was elected to the administrative committee of the Central Sarekat Islam (CSI) where he henceforth allied himself closely with Tjokroaminoto and Gunawan against the radical wing of the party based in Semarang.

18 The "Afdeling B Affair" concerned the discovery of an alleged secret society within the Sarekat Islam in Garut in the Priangan in 1919. The so-called "Afdeling B" was unearthed after a violent incident in which a prominent member of the group, Haji Hasan, was killed by the police. See Noer, *Modernist Muslim Movement*, pp. 195-97; J. Th. Petrus Blumberger, *De Nationalistische Beweging in Nederlandsch-Indië* (Haarlem: Tjeenk Willink, 1931), pp. 69-70; Robert Van Niel, *The Emergence of the Modern Indonesian Elite* (The Hague: van Hoeve, 1960), pp. 148-51; Yong Mun Cheong, *Conflicts within the Prijaji World of the Parahyangan in West Java 1914-1927*, Field Report Series No. 1 (Singapore: Institute of Southeast Asian Studies, January 1973), pp. 21-27; an extensive collection of documents from the Dutch archives on the "Afdeling B" is included in R. C. Kwantes, *De Ontwikkeling van de Nationalistische Beweging in Nederlandsch-Indië*, 1, 1917-20 (Groningen: Tjeenk Willink, 1975), pp. 136-97, 209-12. Several hundred members of the Sarekat Islam were arrested in the wake of the affair, and Dutch inquiries extended to Banten. The affair also led to the exodus of a considerable part of the SI membership from the organization, especially those in government employ. In Banten many junior civil servants and teachers left at this time.

enjoy a shadowy existence. Here leadership was provided by prominent local ulama, whose attitude towards the government was one of marked hostility. By contrast the secular leaders of the Sarekat Islam, and especially Hasan Djajadiningrat, saw the Sarekat Islam as a reformist organization that could win significant reforms by putting pressure on the government and working alongside it. This strategy met with little success at either the national or local level, and the organization proved singularly incapable of ameliorating peasant grievances.

By the end of 1919 the Sarekat Islam entered a period of serious decline. With the close of the First World War and the threat of social revolution in Europe receding, the colonial government felt increasingly unwilling to compromise, and in the ensuing crackdown many Sarekat Islam leaders began to turn to religious matters as a basis for the organization, partly to avoid trouble with the Dutch authorities. H.O. S. Tjokroaminoto, the most prominent Sarekat Islam leader, supported this line, which found support too from Haji Agus Salim and from Haji Fachruddin, the leader of the modernist Moslem educational and social welfare organization, Muhammadiyah.[19] The modernists advocated the purification of Indonesian Islam from local traditions and its adjustment to the requirements of the time. This development was anathema to the traditionalist or *kolot* Moslems of Banten and found no response in the region. The Muhammadiyah's careful avoidance of anything that smacked of political radicalism was viewed with open contempt in Bantenese quarters.

But it was not only the Sarekat Islam's growing concern to avoid radicalism[20] which met with disapproval in Banten. The Muhammadiyah,

---

19 On the decline of the Sarekat Islam after 1919 see van Niel, *Emergence*, pp. 157, 199-210; see also the report by J. J. Schrieke, the government spokesman in the Volksraad to the Governor-General, A. C. de Graeff, October 12, 1927, in R. C. Kwantes, *De Ontwikkeling van de Nationalistische Beweging in Nederlandsch-Indië*, 2 (Groningen: Wolters-Noordhoff, 1978), pp. 630-34. On the Sarekat Islam in Banten see P. A. A. Djajadiningrat, *Herrineringen* (Amsterdam: Kolff, 1936), pp. 285-90; series of articles by Hasan Djajadiningrat entitled "De Politieke Stroomingen In Bantam," *De Taak* [Amsterdam], January 28; February 4, 11, 18, 25; March 25, April 8, 1922.

20 On the swing by the Moslem trading class from the Sarekat Islam to Muhammadiyah, Benda notes, "Many people felt attracted to it [the Muhammadiyah] because it did not propagate attacks on others, not even on Christians, or agitate against imperialism." H.J. Benda, *The Crescent and the Rising Sun: Indonesian Islam under the Japanese Occupation 1942-45* (The Hague: van Hoeve, 1958), pp. 45-46; see also p. 56. On the conservative character of the Muhammadiyah see Ch. van der Plas, "Neutraliseering en bestrijding van revolutionaire propaganda," in Kwantes,

it will be recalled, sought above all to purge Indonesian Islam of its local traditions, a development that was viewed with the greatest hostility in Banten where much of the strength of Islam lay precisely in its close connections with local traditions, passions, and hierarchies. The death of Hasan Djajadiningrat merely served to hasten the antipathy felt in the Sarekat Islam in Banten towards the new developments which found no effective advocate in the region.

This disillusionment with the changed direction of the Sarekat Islam led the party's local Bantenese sections to adopt a strictly neutral line in the quarrel which developed within the organization between the conservative leadership based in Yogyakarta and the PKI radicals in Semarang led by Semaun. Indeed such was Bantenese resentment towards Tjokroaminoto and the rest of the Yogyakarta leaders that, when the split between Semarang and Yogyakarta became absolute in 1923, the Bantenese ulama urged the replacement of Tjokroaminoto by the PKI leaders Alimin and Musso.[21]

Nationally and in Banten, the early 1920s saw the peasantry drifting away from the Sarekat Islam as quickly as they had joined it at an earlier stage. They had found that the Sarekat Islam was unable to redress their considerable grievances. In Banten the failure of the nationalist organization found them turning again to more traditional forms of protest. Where the Sarekat Islam survived, it either adopted a militant stance, as in Labuan and Menes under the leadership of Haji Achmad Chatib, or, as in Cilegon, it became a virtual secret society with distinct criminal overtones.[22] Elsewhere in the region the organization simply withered away and a political vacuum existed which was eventually filled by the Communist Party.

The Beginnings of Communism in Banten

The origins of Indonesian communism can be traced to the founding, in May 1914, of the Indische Sociaal Democratische Vereeniging (ISDV) by

---

Ontwikkeling van de Nationalistische Beweging, 2, pp. 712-13.

21 McVey, *Rise*, pp. 302-303; "Kort Verslag van de Bestuursvergadering van de PKI ende SI, 3 March 1923," Mailr 286x/23.

22 See "Bantam Report," p. 28; MvO, W. Ch. Thieme, June 1920, pp. 8-9.

the Dutch Marxist, Henk Sneevliet.[23] The ISDV, the first Marxist party in Asia, although at first dominated by Dutch socialists, developed close links with the infant Indonesian labor movement, much of which grew up under the tutelage of the ISDV. In particular the party worked closely with the strongest and oldest Indonesian trade union, the Vereeniging voor Spoor en Tramweg Personeel (VSTP), the railway and tram workers' union. The VSTP formed the proletarian core of first the ISDV and later of the Indonesian Communist Party, founded in May 1920.

The need to establish bonds with the wider mass of the Indonesian population, however, led the ISDV to pursue from 1916 a "bloc-within" strategy inside the Sarekat Islam. This strategy, the first concrete example of a Marxist party attempting to infiltrate another party and form cells within it as a means of developing its own propaganda and contacts among the masses, was to pay large dividends for the ISDV and later for the PKI. The strategy was possible largely because of the decentralized character of the Sarekat Islam, resulting from the refusal of the Netherlands East Indies government to sanction a national organization. As a consequence of the Marxist infiltration of the organization, several local branches of the Sarekat Islam fell wholly under the sway of the Semarang-based ISDV. It was several years before a coherent right-wing trend emerged in the Sarekat Islam, and the PKI was finally forced to abandon the "bloc-within" policy only in 1921.

The ISDV itself never established a branch in Banten, although two members of its executive committee did live in the area, Hasan Djajadiningrat and the Dutch Marxist, J. C. Stam. Despite their presence, there is little evidence that either of them made any concerted effort to win the Banten Sarekat Islam to the radical positions propounded by the Marxists in Sernarang. Hasan Djajadiningrat's own political views were decidedly moderate and not all that distinct from the liberal Dutch "Ethici"

---

23 On the early years of the ISDV see McVey, Rise, pp. 7-75; Poeze, Tan Malaka, pp. 114-66; Djamaluddin Tamin, Sedjarah PKI (mimeo, n.d.), 100 pp.; Djamaluddin Tamin, Speech to Persatuan Pemuda Indonesia (Tokyo: mimeo, April 1967), 13 pp.; Max Perthus, Henk Sneevliet: Revolutionair Socialist in Europa en Azie (Nijmegen: Sun, 1976), pp. 89-201; Fritjof Tichelman, Henk Sneevliet: Een Politieke Biografie (Amsterdam: Van Gennep, 1974), pp. 22-26; Mintz, "Marxism in Indonesia," pp. 176-80; Lembaga Sedjarah PKI, Pemberontakan Nasional Pertama (Jakarta: Jajasan Pembaruan, 1961), pp. 34-50; Michael Williams, "Sneevliet—A Comintern Odyssey," New Left Review, 123 (September-October 1980), pp. 81-91.

reformers. He belonged to the minority reformist wing of the ISDV, and in 1919 he resigned, declaring himself a follower of the German reformist socialist, Lassalle rather than Marx.[24]

Stam, however, adhered to the revolutionary position proposed by Sneevliet and most of the ISDV leadership. He worked as a schoolteacher in Banten from 1916 to 1919, first in Serang and then in Rangkasbitung.[25] Stam was a prominent member of the ISDV and was often visited in Serang by other ISDV leaders such as Sneevliet, Brandstedter, and Bergsma. He was a frequent contributor to the party journal, *Het Vrije Woord,* and in April 1918 founded the socialist teachers' paper, *De Indische Volksschool,* with B. Coster and W. Snel. When the PKI was formed in May 1920, he became a member of its executive committee and was later proposed by the party as its candidate for the Volksraad (Peoples' Assembly).[26]

From the point of view of his impact on Banten, however, Stam seems to have achieved little. He did occasionally address meetings of the Sarekat Islam on important national issues, such as the trial of Sneevliet in September 1917.[27] Stam himself was acutely aware of his political isolation in the region and tried to get round this by establishing debating clubs in Serang and Rangkasbitung. The clubs attracted members among junior priyayi, schoolteachers, and local officials of the railways, pawnhouse, and irrigation services. However, I have not been able to trace any link between the clubs and the later growth of the PKI in Banten. In November 1919 Stam was transferred to Tuban in Central Java; two years later he left Indonesia for good.

Stam was not the only important Dutch Communist to have lived in Banten. Some years later G.J. van Munster was appointed a teacher at the

---

24 On Hasan Djajadiningrat's moderate political views see McVey, Rise, pp. 302 and 370, n. 17; see also Djajadiningrat, "Politieke Stroomingen"; van Niel, *Emergence,* p. 128; D. M. G. Koch, *Verantwoording: Een Halve Eeuw in Indonesie* (Bandung: van Hoeve, 1956), p. 101.

25 On Stam see Perthus, *Henk Sneevliet,* pp. 165, 172, 176, 188, 193, 207, 479, 483; see also the document in Mailr 490x/19, Vb October 22, 1921 Z11/62.

26 Stam left Indonesia in 1921. The following year he attended the Third Congress of the Comintern in Moscow, representing the PKI. See Perthus, *Henk Sneevliet,* p. 483 n. 175; Vb February 17, 1922 T1/10.

27 Perthus, *Henk Sneevliet,* p. 165; see also Vb April 21, 1921 P5. Although Stam seems to have had little contact with religious leaders in Banten, it was later reported that, while teaching in Banjarmasin, he had been working with local haji to convince them the PKI was not opposed to Islam or the SI. See Mailr 80x/ Vb November 5, 1925 B16; also Mailr 595x/1922.

Opleidings-School voor Inlandsche Ambtenaren (OSVIA) in Serang.[28] But van Munster, although a member of the PKI, was even more isolated in Banten than Stam had been. His only real contacts seem to have been with his students, on whom he evidently made a great impression.[29] In October 1924 he was expelled from Indonesia by the Dutch authorities, earning the distinction of being the last Dutch Communist to be thrown out of the country.[30]

Although the ISDV had not established a branch in Banten, the railway workers' union, the VSTP, had.[31] The VSTP held a public meeting in Labuan in July 1922 at which the main speaker was the PKI leader, Semaun. The following year the VSTP launched a railway strike throughout Java in support of a claim for better wages and conditions for its members. Several meetings were held in Banten during the course of the strike, a number of them addressed by the VSTP chairman, Sugono, attracting large audiences.[32]

The failure of the 1923 railway strike led to a wave of victimization against those considered to be militant activists by the Dutch authorities and employers.[33] Among those sacked was a Bantenese clerk working at the Tanah Abang railway station in Batavia, Raden Oesadiningrat. Unemployed, Oesadiningrat, who was a distant relative of Achmad Djajadiningrat, the Regent of Serang, returned to his native Pandeglang where he found employment with the VSTP as a full-time official. Although there was no PKI branch, or even membership in Banten, Oesadiningrat did organize three public meetings in 1924 at which prominent PKI leaders spoke. Ironically, Oesadiningrat, who was instrumental in these modest attempts by the PKI to recruit a following in Banten, was eventually to play an important role as a spy and police agent in the suppression of the

---

28 Mailr 789x/24, Vb December 22, 1924 T17; interview with Haji Gogo Sanjadirdja, May 1976, Serang. The informant was a former pupil of van Munster at the Serang OSVIA.
29 Interviews, Serang, 1975-76.
30 Besluit 1x October 1, 1924, Mailr 789x/24, Vb December 22, 1924 T17. See also Vb May 13, 1922, Vb May 1, 1923 W5; *De Banten Bode*, October 4, 1924; McVey, *Rise*, pp. 253, 454 n. 5, 471 n. 70. Van Munster was the former Director of the Teachers' Training College in Blitar, then Adjunct Inspector of Native Education in Aceh. His post in Serang was his last before his expulsion from Indonesia.
31 "Bantam Report," p. 29, gives the membership of the VSTP in Banten as 240.
32 Letter of Procureur-Generaal to Governor- General, March 2, 1923 in Mailr 216x/23, Vb October 1, 1923 E14.
33 McVey, Rise, pp. 146-54; *Pemberontakan Nasional Pertama*, pp. 39-40.

1926 insurrection.[34]

After the complete rupture between the PKI and the Sarekat Islam in 1923, the Communist Party established its own mass organization, the Sarekat Rakjat. Although the Sarekat Islam in Banten, or what was left of it, was hostile to Tjokroaminoto and Salim's leadership of the Sarekat Islam, the PKI made no attempt to court the Bantenese Sarekat Islam or to establish branches of the Sarekat Rakjat in the region. In August 1924 Oesadiningrat did chair a meeting in Pandeglang organized by the VSTP, apparently with the intention of establishing the Sarekat Rakjat in Banten, but from police reports it appears that nothing came of it.[35]

In October 1924 Oesadiningrat made another attempt to set up a branch of the Sarekat Rakjat and invited the PKI leaders, Alimin and Musso, to speak at inaugural meetings. The two leaders spoke on October 12 at a meeting in Pandeglang attended by only fourteen people. The following day a meeting at Kadomas drew a crowd of only nine. Nothing further came of the attempt to establish the Sarekat Rakjat in the region, and soon afterwards Oesadiningrat left Banten for Central Java to return only in 1926, this time as a police agent.[36]

Such were the meager beginnings of the PKI in Banten. Given such an unpromising start, the rapid growth of the party within a comparatively short period was unexpected, and it certainly took the Dutch administration completely by surprise. At the end of 1924 a government report found that there were only two known members of the Communist Party in the residency of Banten.[37] Only twelve months later party membership was to number several thousand and was to grow even more in 1926.

This startling change in the PKP's fortunes was brought about by a small number of men who moved to Banten in 1925. Some were Bantenese who had joined the PKI in other areas of Java, others were itinerant artisans,

---

34   Report of Governor of West Java, W. P. Hillen, to Governor-General Fock, March 8, 1926, G5/7/10 Mailr 296x/26.

35   Ibid.

36   Ibid. Interview Agus Sirad, November 12, 1975, Jakarta. Agus Sirad was a *mantri politie* in Pandeglang in 1924. In 1975 he recalled: "I was detailed to follow Alimin and Musso on their arrival in Pandeglang. They arrived on the evening train. I thought at first they were well-dressed merchants. Alimin was short and Musso fat; they reminded me of Laurel and Hardy."

37   "Opgave van Ambtenaren en Beambten in Nederlandsch-Indischen Staatsdienst," Mailr 651x/24, Vb January 5, 1925 F3.

and a few were full-time party propagandists dispatched at the behest of the executive committee to establish a section there.

One of the Bantenese who returned to his home area in 1925 was Tubagus Alipan. Born in 1902 in Pandeglang, Tb. Alipan was the son of a minor official and had attended the HIS (Dutch language school for Indonesians) in Pandeglang. In 1917 he went to live in Temanggung in Central Java and eventually found work there as a printer.[38] He became active in the Printers' Union (Sarekat Buruh Cetak), and in 1921 joined the PKI. Two years later he became a propagandist for the party and was responsible for trade union work in the Temanggung area. In 1925, according to his own story, he was requested by the PKI chairman, Darsono, to return to Banten to assist in establishing a section of the party. As he played an important role in the development of the revolutionary movement, it is interesting to recall some of his life history in his own words.

> "My first political experience was when I was still young and living in Pandeglang. Tjokroaminoto came to the town to address a meeting of the Sarekat Islam in 1916. I remember the excitement not only of us youngsters, but throughout the town. Even though at the time I understood little of the political content of the meeting, Tjokroaminoto to us was almost a superhuman personality and symbolized the awakening of the Indonesian people...
>
> "Temanggung was a very different place from Banten. It was much more open and I rapidly became politicized by the currents of the time. I began working in a printing plant there and this became my vocation. The conditions of the workers at that time were of course very poor. To try and improve matters, I established with some other comrades a mutual benefit society, 'Rukun Temanggung.' Soon afterwards, I joined the Printers' Union and later the PKI."[39]

---

38 Interview Tb. Alipan, Pandeglang, February 18 and 25, March 10, 1976; Ali-pan's notes entitled "Riwayat singkat pribadi," in my possession. Temanggung seems to have been a particularly active PKI area; see McVey, *Rise*, p. 332.
39 Interview Tb. Alipan.

Alipan returned to Banten with Puradisastra, the future chairman of the Banten section of the PKI, in August 1925. Puradisastra was a Sundanese from Banjar, near Ciamis in the Priangan.[40] He had joined the PKI in 1923 and worked for the party in West Java and also in Bengkulu in Sumatra, an area where many Bantenese worked as migrant laborers. Puradisastra himself had married a Bantenese woman from Menes. His younger sister, Sukaesih, was one of the few prominent women members of the PKI in the 1920s. In 1924 Puradisastra had worked closely with the PKI leader Musso in trying to reactivate the labor unions in Batavia, particularly the Printers' Union and the Drivers' Union.

Puradisastra and Alipan were assisted in their work by a number of other Bantenese who had become PKI activists, the most prominent of whom was Achmad Bassaif.[41] Bassaif was born in Serang in 1903, the son of an Arab father and a Bantenese mother. His father was a comparatively wealthy trader and Bassaif himself was educated at the Al-Irsjad school in Batavia. He was recruited into the PKI by Puradisastra. Bassaif became an enormous asset to the PKI because of his background; he was fluent in Arabic and had a deep knowledge of Islam and its scriptures, credentials which were to serve the party well in 1925 and 1926. He quickly became a full-time activist and chairman of the subsection of the party in Jembatan Lima, a neighborhood of Batavia heavily populated with Bantenese. In 1925 he became chairman of the PKI subsection in Tangerang, where he successfully allayed many local suspicions regarding the PKI's alleged hostility towards Islam.[42] In late 1925 he returned to Banten to help with the establishment of the PKT's thirty-seventh section.

Another early member of the Banten Communist group was Mohammed Abdu Rachmat.[43] Like Tb. Alipan, he was a printer by profession. Born in Ceribon, he had joined the PKI in 1923 and two years later moved to Serang, where he began to work on *De Banten Bode*, a newspaper founded in September 1924 by Charles M. Fritz.[44]

---

40 Interviews Tje Mamat, Serang, May-June 1976.

41 Interviews Achmad Bassaif, April 14, June 6, 16, 1976.

42 Ibid. See also *Njala*, September 6, November 7, 1925.

43 Interviews Mohammed Abdu Rachmat, Serang, December 14, 1975, January 5, 1976.

44 Ibid. The first issue of *De Banten Bode* appeared on September 17, 1924. The paper was a weekly with articles in Dutch and Indonesian and appeared until 1942. A full run of the newspaper is kept in the National Museum in Jakarta.

"Not long after I arrived in Banten, Alipan and Puradisastra came to see me, having been given my name by a comrade from Ceribon. They spoke about the need to develop PKI activity in Banten and that I should assist in setting up a party cell among the workers on the newspaper. This I did, together with two other printers on the paper who had secretly joined the party, Ishak, who was from Banten, and Atmodihardjo, who was Javanese. My own political influence was quite limited as I am not santri and there was little political work for me outside Serang."[45]

Abdu Rachmat, Atmodihardjo, and Ishak worked in close collaboration with Djarkasih, another of the early Communists to be sent by the PKI to Banten. Like Puradisastra, Djarkasih was Sundanese and had been active in the party in the Priangan. Djarkasih moved to Serang in July 1925 and opened a cycle-repair shop in the market. Here many of the first meetings of the small group of Serang Communists were held in July and August 1925. Abdu Rachmat recalls those early days:

"At first we worked entirely underground, partly because we wished to establish a presence without the police being aware of our existence but also because we were apprehensive about what form party work should take in Banten given that the area is a devoutly Moslem region."[46]

In this respect the group was to experience its most serious teething problem with the behavior of its own leader, Puradisastra. The future chairman of the Banten section of the PKI openly told those he encountered that he was an atheist, and he committed the cardinal sin for Banten of drinking coffee in public during Ramadan (the fasting month).[47]

Puradisastra's somewhat intemperate behavior was curbed by the timely arrival in Banten of Achmad Bassaif, whom we have already met, and another PKI propagandist with a distinctly Islamic background,

---

45   Interview Abdu Rachmat.
46   Ibid.
47   "Bantam Report," p. 45.

Hasanuddin, who came from West Sumatra.[48] Evidently the PKI leadership in Batavia took rather more care in selecting its propagandists than in its choice of chairmen of local sections. Whatever the case, the combination of Puradisastra, Bassaif, and Hasanuddin, together with the small group of Serang Communists, most of whom we have now met, was to prove remarkably effective in the closing months of 1925 in building the PKI's thirty-seventh section.

But before we look in greater depth at the development of the Communist movement in Banten, it is important to recall the context of the PKI's work in the region. Bassaif sets the tone for us,

"The keynote of our work was agitation. In Banten everything possible was done to incite the people. The PKI's work there was different from other areas. It was the last residency of Java where the party established a section and this move virtually coincided with the Prambanan decision [to launch an insurrection]. Thus, in Banten, the work of building a Communist base had to coincide with preparations for the coming revolt. In the process the leadership, after some initial hestiation, naturally gave great emphasis to the latter rather than to developing a solid core of Communist cadres.

"Naturally a most important aspect of our work was the recruitment of influential persons, especially militant ulama, but also jawara, to the revolutionary cause. Our work was enormously aided by the great chasm of mistrust that existed in Banten between the people and the government. The movement grew faster than any of us imagined."[49]

The PKI's Road to Revolt

Bassaif's remarks are a good point at which to take stock of the situation of the Indonesian Communist Party on the eve of the commencement of its activities in Banten in August 1925. By this date the PKI had eclipsed the Sarekat Islam as the major political force on the Indonesian scene. From

---

48   Interview Tje Mamat.
49   Interview Achmad Bassaif, April 18, 1976.

its Third Congress in June 1924 it had, moreover, increasingly isolated itself from other elements in the Indonesian nationalist movement. The party's experiment with bloc-within strategy inside the Sarekat Islam had long since been abandoned by its virtual expulsion at the October 1921 Sarekat Islam conference.[50]

For some time thereafter the PKI still attempted to maintain a grip on many of the Sarekat Islam's local branches, especially those in urban areas. As a result, the Sarekat Islam became torn between the radical "red" (*merah*) PKI leadership in Semarang and the moderate "white" (*putih*) leadership in Yogyakarta. This conflict found little reflection in Banten, partly because of the marked distrust of the Bantenese towards the Yogyakarta modernists, but also because the Sarekat Islam in the region went into steep decline after 1920. The PKI tried to organize its support in the "red" branches of the SI into a new organization, the Sarekat Rakjat, but this new organization made no impact on Banten.[51]

After its 1921 expulsion from the Sarekat Islam, the PKI concentrated its attention for a time on the urban working class. This renewed interest in the labor movement manifested itself in increased strike activity, culminating in the pawnshop workers' strike of 1922 and the railway workers' stoppage of 1923.[52] The strikes, however, achieved little and led to growing attempts by the colonial authorities to curtail the Communist movement. In particular, some of the PKI's most able leaders, such as Tan Malaka, Bergsma, and Semaun, were expelled from Indonesian in 1922-23.[53]

The difficullties the party had met in organizing labor unions led it from 1923 to turn again to expanding its work in the countryside and also in other areas of Indonesia where it had previously been inactive.[54] In Java, prior to this date, most of the PKI's activities had been concentrated

---

50 McVey, Rise, pp. 103-4; Blumberger, *Communistische*, p. 29; Blumberger, *Nationalitische*, p. 73.
51 On the Sarekat Rakjat, see "Perserikatan Kommunist India. Sarekat Rakjat," report of Adviser for Native Affairs, R. A. Kern, to Governor-General Fock, November 27, 1923 in Kwantes, *Ontwikkeling*, 2, pp. 46-50; S. Dingley, *The Peasants' Movement in Indonesia* (Berlin: Prager, 1926), pp. 39-47. The latter is a critique of PKI policies and, in particular, the absence of any specific program for the peasantry.
52 On the pawnshop workers' strike see McVey, Rise, p. 123; Poeze, *Tan Malaka*, pp. 149-52. On the railway workers' strike see McVey, *Rise*, pp. 146-54; Poeze, *Tan Malaka*, pp. 235-36.
53 Tamin, *Sedjarah PKI*, p. 10; McVey, Rise, pp. 123, 153.
54 McVey, *Rise*, pp. 181-83.

in the Central and East provinces of the island. The "capital of Indonesian Communism" had been Semarang, and the PKI's organization in West Java was comparatively underdeveloped. In March 1923 a special congress of the PKI and of the "Red" Sarekat Islam had been held in Bandung[55] and increased efforts were made to expand party activities in the region. The same year two men who were later to become important PKI leaders, Alimin and Musso, were released from prison having served four-year sentences for their alleged involvement in the "Afdeling B" affair of 1919.[56]

On their release from detention, Alimin and Musso joined the PKI and began to play an important role in the increased party efforts in West Java. Alimin became active in organizing seamen and dockers in Batavia's port, Tanjung Priok,[57] and Musso played a crucial role in reorganizing the Batavia PKI from March 1924.[58] Throughout 1924 the PKI expanded in West Java, and after the party congress in June of that year the PKI headquarters was transferred from Semarang to Batavia.[59] At the same time, a Sundanese party official from Bandung, Winanta, became chairman of the PKI.[60]

The June 1924 congress was marked by a distinct swing to the left for the PKI, and this trend was confirmed by a special conference of the party in December 1924 at Kutagede, near Yogyakarta. The conference decided to disband the Sarekat Rakjat, absorbing its membership into the PKI and virtually condemning the party to a course that could only end in armed revolt.[61] Under the direction and influence of an executive now dominated by Aliarcham, the party effectively abandoned the principle of "democratic centralism" in favor of federative centralism and reached a

---

55 *Pemberontakan Nasional Pertama*, p. 45; Poeze, *Tan Malaka*, p. 235; McVey, *Rise*, p. 155.

56 Tamin, *Sedjarah PKI*, p. 3; McVey, *Rise*, pp. 41, 50. Interview Tje Mamat.

57 Interview Achmad Bassaif; McVey, *Rise*, p. 168.

58 Interviews Achmad Bassaif and Tb. Alipan.

59 Lembaga Sedjarah PKI, *40 Tahun PKI* (Jakarta: Jajasan Pembaruan, 1960), pp. 20-23; see also the reports in "Communisme. Negende PKI—Congres," Kwantes, *Ontwikkeling*, 2, pp. 151-68; Tamin, *Sedjarah PKI*, pp. 14-15; Sudijono Djojoprajitno, *PKI—SI BAR contra Tan Malaka* (Jakarta: Jajasan Massa, 1962), p. 18.

60 McVey, *Rise*, p. 193.

61 Ibid., p. 262; Djojoprajitno, PKI-SIBAR, p. 19; Tamin, *Sedjarah PKI*, p. 15. See also report by R. A. Kern, Adviser for Native and Islamic Affairs to Governor-General Fock, January 3, 1925, in Kwantes, *Ontwikkeling*, 2, pp. 264-67; Dingley, *Peasants' Movement*, pp. 42-43; and reports on this conference in Mailr 74x/25. There were no representatives from Banten at the conference.

decision to establish an illegal organization.[62]

The party's new direction was further confirmed by a meeting of the PKI leadership in March 1925.[63] As a result of decisions taken at this meeting there was now almost no possibility of turning away from the path of armed revolt. Local units of the party were to be granted greater autonomy and to be allowed to act independently, as long as their decisions were in line with the PKI constitution and by-laws. These units were to be based on cells of five members who, when sufficiently trained, would recruit others to the organization.[64] In order to avoid the authorities' increasingly repressive measures, the party leadership advised its branches to substitute small closed meetings for open public ones.[65] The PKI was to be divided into major territorial units that would be responsible to headquarters in Batavia. Former party branches would become subsections of these new units, which were to expand in number to seventy-five.

One of the most interesting and relevant decisions to emerge from the March 1925 meeting as far as Banten was concerned was that "adventurist elements" were to be recruited into the party. This decision was strongly argued by Alimin, whose previous involvement with the "Afdeling B" and with Batavia labor unions we have already noted. During his work with seamen and dockers in Tanjung Priok, Alimin almost certainly came into contact with Bantenese jawara gangs who were active in labor recruitment and smuggling.[66] Alimin argued that such elements could serve the party as well as fight against it, as they had done when they were enrolled into the right-wing gangs of the Sarekat Hidjau.[67] They were

---

62 McVey, *Rise*, p. 274; Poeze, *Tan Malaka*, pp. 265-67.
63 Interview Achmad Bassaif; McVey, *Rise*, pp. 298-99.
64 Interviews Achmad Bassaif and Tje Mamat; McVey, *Rise*, p. 274.
65 Report of Procureur-Generaal, D. G. Wolterbeek Muller, to Governor-General Fock, August 14, 1925, and report of Procureur-Generaal, H. G. P. Duyfjes, to Governor-General de Graeff, November 27, 1926 in Kwantes, *Ontwikkeling*, 2, pp. 330-46 and pp. 480-94; McVey, Rise, p. 291. Many reports on PKI strategy and tactics in 1925 are contained in Mailr 7x/Vb June 21, 1927 A 10. PKI strategy after the Kutagede conference of December 1924 was vehemently criticized by *Tan Malaka, inter alia* in his "Semangat Moeda," pp. 57-65, cited by Poeze, Tan Malaka, p. 296; see also McVey, *Rise*, pp. 305, 316-19.
66 Interviews Tb. Alipan and Haji Solichin, Serang, April 1976.
67 See Blumberger, *Communistische*, p. 49; McVey, *Rise*, p. 295. On the utilization of lawless elements by the Sarekat Hidjau see Heather Sutherland, *The Making of a Bureaucratic Elite* (Singapore: Heinemann, 1979), p. 95. The Sarekat Hidjau was an organization formed by priyayi in the Priangan to combat the growth of the PKI.

at present disaffected from most political organizations but they had a healthy contempt for authority and the law and, when it came down to it, knew how to look after themselves.

This latter decision was to have important repercussions in Banten. The region was notorious for its unruly elements. The Sarekat Islam, under Hasan Djajadiningrat's guidance, had sought to exclude them, though not entirely with success. The PKI, on the other hand, now deliberately chose to recruit them. Although this decision had important repercussions and results elsewhere, its significance in Banten was far greater, for at the time of the March 1925 meeting, no party organization existed in the region and thus there was no corpus of experienced party militants who would perhaps have been able to integrate the "adventurist elements" without allowing them too much influence on party structure and tactics.

When the PKI began to establish a section in Banten in September 1925, it was, then, already committed to a strategy that could only culminate in armed revolt. Faced with the dismal failure of the strike wave of 1925 this became even more inevitable as the labor unions, with the exception of the VSTP, simply collapsed.[68] However, as the party embarked on this disastrous course more and more of its most capable leaders were removed from the scene. By the end of 1925 Darsono, Aliarcham, and Mardjohan had been expelled from Indonesia or were under arrest.[69] As Ruth McVey has aptly noted: "[The] removal of top PKI leaders placed the party in the hands of men whose desire to create a revolution was by no means matched by their ability to plan one."[70]

The decision to organize an armed revolt was taken at a secret conference of the remaining PKI leadership at Prambanan near Yogyakarta in December 1925, but, before we come to that fateful decision and its outcome, let us return to the development of the PKI in Banten.

Rukun Asli

The PKI's early moves in Banten, Puradisastra's coffee drinking excepted,

---

68   McVey, *Rise*, p. 310; *Pemberontakan Nasional Pertama*, pp. 46-47.
69   Kwantes, *Ontwikkeling*, 2, pp. 365-81; Tamin, *Sedjarah PKI*, pp. 14 and 21. See also Tamin's speech "Persatuan Pemuda Indonesia," p. 2.
70   McVey, *Rise*, p. 308.

were marked by a genuine subtlety and delicacy in handling Bantenese susceptibilities and sensitivities. Yet, with the exception of Achmad Bassaif, Tb. Alipan, and Tb. Hilman, most of the early PKI leaders in Banten were not local people. Despite this considerable handicap, in a region notorious for its distrust of outsiders, in a comparatively short period of time the PKI successfully implanted itself in Bantenese soil. At the same time the PKI conveyed to its Bantenese membership the not easily accepted notion that they were part of a nationwide movement against Dutch colonial oppression.

This was a significant departure from earlier protest movements in Banten. The Cilegon uprising of 1888, for example, was local both in scope and leadership. Indeed it was largely limited to the Serang regency.[71] Even the advent of the Sarekat Islam in Banten did not mark such a distinct change as did the PKI in 1925-26. The Sarekat Islam's leadership was local in origin and, with the exception of Hasan Djajadiningrat, had few connections with the Central Sarekat Islam and only a limited awareness of being part of a national movement. The virtual rupture of relations between the Sarekat Islam in Banten and the CSI after 1920 amply demonstrated the latter point. Later developments in the Sarekat Islam, such as the split between Yogyakarta and Semarang, the increasingly religious focus of the CSI, and the growth of new organizations like the Sarekat Rakjat and the Sarekat Hidjau, had almost no impact in Banten.

The growth of the PKI in Banten was effectively to break the political isolation of the region while at the same time developing some consciousness among party members of belonging to a national movement. One should not underestimate the significance of this point, because much of the success of the insurrectionary movement that culminated in the November 1926 uprising can be attributed to the rebels' widespread feeling that they were merely one front of a national revolutionary struggle against colonial rule. They were in that sense a perceptible development from traditional protest movements towards new forms of protest, although, as we shall see, their movement contained many traditional elements.[72]

---

71 Sartono Kartodirdjo, *The Peasants' Revolt of Banten in 1888* (The Hague: Nijhoff, 1966), pp. 233, 237.
72 In this sense Shelton Stromquist is right to stress the break that the 1926 uprising marks with

Banten, as will be recalled, was the last residency of Java where a section of the PKI was formed. In the neighboring Tangerang area of Batavia residency a PKI subsection was set up in early 1925 under the able chairmanship of Achmad Bassaif.[73] The PKI had also developed a strong subsection in the Batavia neighborhood of Jembatan Lima, an area of the capital where Bantenese traditionally congregated.[74] Bassaif and Puradisastra had been instrumental in establishing the PKI in Jembatan Lima and had successfully recruited many Bantenese living there who were later to be dispatched to their home region as propagandists.

According to Bassaif, the Batavia leadership of the PKI decided in June 1925 that a rapid spread of PKI activities to Banten was an urgent priority.[75] The implementation of this decision was assigned to Puradisastra and Bassaif who enlisted as lieutenants Tb. Alipan, Tb. Hilman, and Djarkasih. In the next two months the group moved to Serang and began establishing a network of contacts there.[76] Alipan recalled this early and difficult period of organization,

> "It was strange for me to return to Banten after many years absence. I had regarded myself as a Communist for several years and was no longer a practicing Moslem. In Java I had not used my title (Tubagus) because such things were clearly feudal and 'kolot' [old-fashioned, conservative]. In Banten, however, Bass [Bassaif] would insist on Hilman and myself using our titles. 'You know full well what the title Tubagus means for the Bantenese,' he would say. 'We must adapt ourselves to the way the people think and then see what we can do from there.'"[77]

---

earlier local revolts against colonial rule. See his "The Communist Uprising of 1926 in Indonesia: A Reinterpretation," *Journal of South East Asian History,* 18, 2 (1967), pp. 189-200.

73   Interview Achmad Bassaif.

74   *Njala* [Spark], the newspaper of the Batavia PKI, reported meetings of 600 party members in Jembatan Lima in October 1925. See the issue of October 23, 1925. *Njala* was published between September 1925 and April 30, 1926. A complete run of the newspaper is kept in the National Museum in Jakarta.

75   Interview Achmad Bassaif.

76   Interview Tb. Alipan and Mohammed Abdu Rachmat. Tb. Hilman was already living in Serang at the time of the start of PKI activities.

77   Interview Tb. Alipan.

Bassaif's advice to Alipan was indeed sound and, more importantly, it was to pay handsome dividends in the following months.

Fortunately for the PKI leaders in Banten, the executive of the party, as we have seen, had decided in 1925 to grant considerable autonomy to local sections. Rigid doctrinaire stances, particularly on such highly sensitive issues as the relationship between communism and Islam, were to be avoided. Instead considerable attention and energies were to be devoted to the matters that directly concerned the masses, their daily difficulties and grievances. Moreover, because of the great importance of personal leadership in rural society in securing a popular following, the party leadership set great store on recruiting local notables.[78] This was to produce problems later, as those brought into the party often proved difficult to control, but at least in the short run the results were wholly beneficial to the PKI in Banten and elsewhere.

The first recruits to the PKI in Banten,however, came from a more orthodox base of support for a left-wing party, the printing workers on *De Banten Bode* in Serang. Three of their number, Atmodihardjo, Ishak, and Abdu Rachmat were to become important local leaders of the PKI. These men, together with seven or eight other workers from the Fritz printing works, Tb. Hilman, Tb. Alipan, Alirachman, an employee of Hasan Djajadiningrat's widow, Lee Eng Hock, a local Chinese trader, would meet secretly with Bassaif and Puradisastra at the cycle shop owned by Djarkasih in Serang market.[79] The meetings discussed,among other things, how best to seek Bantenese support in the PKI's struggle with the colonial government.

As an outcome of these early meetings, not only did Alipan and Hilman revert to using their "feudal" titles but they set about contacting other

---

78   See McVey, *Rise*, p. 277; interview Achmad Bassaif.

79   According to Haji Solichin (interview Serang, March 6, 1976), Djarkasih's bicycle repair shop was the venue for the first secret meetings of the PKI in Banten. Most of the early members were workers at the Fritz Printing Works, the publisher of the local newspaper, *De Banten Bode*. In addition to Djarkasih, the original members appear to have been Ishak, Atmodihardjo, Solichin, Arman, Tb. Alipan, Alirachman, Abdu Rachmat, and Lee Eng Hock. After a requisite number of cadres were trained, "Rukun Asli" was established. "Rukun Asli" was variously described by ex-PKI members to the writer as a *kedok* (mask) or *batu loncaton* (stepping-stone). Two other early members of the secret PKI in Banten, Tb. Hilman and Tb. Arif, put themselves forward, unsuccessfully, as candidates for the Regency Council of Serang in August 1925. See De Banten Bode, August 22 and September 26, 1925. See also *Njala*, September 14, 1925.

descendants of the former Sultans of Banten, with a view to petitioning the Dutch Governor-General to obtain pensions. Indeed so successful were these intrepid Communists in arguing for the rights of disinherited nobles that no fewer than 200 of them signed a petition in August 1925 asking that all bearers of the title "tubagus" (male descendants) and "*ratu*" (female descendants) be granted pensions. Such were the beginnings of communism in Banten.[80]

Soon after this novel attempt at gaining support, Tb. Hilman, and Ishak, a printing worker on *De Banten Bode*, announced the establishment of a mutual benefit and burial society, Rukun Asli (Original Harmony). The first meeting of the new association took place in the village of Kramatwatu, half way on the road between Serang and Cilegon, on August 22, 1925. The choice of Kramatwatu as a venue for the first meeting may not have been fortuitous, for it had been one of the villages most involved in the Cilegon uprising of 1888, and many of the sons of the rebels still lived there.[81] Some eighty people attended the first meeting chaired by Ishak, at which Tb. Hilman also spoke. The meeting elected as chairman, H. Achmad Noer, a clerk in Serang who had recently secretly joined the PKI.[82]

Members of the new association were to be charged an entry fee of one guilder which could be paid in ten monthly installments. Ishak announced that the primary intention of the new society would be to relieve the hardship caused to members by the deaths of close relatives by meeting funeral expenses. In time it was hoped that the new society would be able to extend the range of benefits available to members so that they would no longer be forced to sell or pawn their belongings in times of hardship. Rukun Asli, Ishak continued, had no political objectives and intended to abide by the laws of the land. Furthermore, the new associations intentions and aims were fully in accord with the precepts

---

80 *De Banten Bode*, August 15, 1925. On the origins of the titles Tubagus and Ratu and other Bantenese titles, see L. W. C. van den Berg, *Rangen en Titels op Java en Madoera*, 2nd ed. (The Hague: Nijhoff, 1902), pp. 17-21.

81 See Sartono, *Peasants' Revolt*, pp. 233-34. On "Rukun Asli," see also the report of W. P. Hillen to Governor-General Fock, March 8, 1926, G5/7/10 Mailr 296x/ 26. To party members the initials RAB (Rukun Asli Banten) were said to mean Revolusi Anak Negeri Banten (Revolt of the People of Banten).

82 Interview Tb. Alipan; *De Banten Bode*, August 29, 1925.

of Islam, for the prophet Mohammed had made no distinction between rich and poor.[83]

The choice of such a platform as "Rukun Asli" to promote PKI aims was not as unusual as it might seem at first. It will be recalled that Tb. Alipan had been instrumental, some years earlier, in establishing a similar society in Temanggung, and the PKI had also used the idea in other areas.[84] Moreover, peasant societies have traditions of forming such associations as a way of coping with the modern world and its demands. The PKI in Banten probably also had in mind that, as recently as 1922, Haji Nawawi of the Cilegon Sarekat Islam had formed a similar society.[85]

It appears that the Rukun Asli soon won popular support in Banten and that a number of religious leaders lent their support to the new organization.[86] Meetings were reportedly held in villages in the Serang area in mosques and *langgar*. In September a serious fire in Batavia, which left many homeless, prompted a large meeting of the Rukun Asli in Serang attended by more than 300 people.[87] The main speech at the meeting was delivered by Ishak, who declared that the tragedy in Batavia underlined the need for the common people to come together to cope with the many adversities that they had to face. Puradisastra himself then spoke, drawing to the attention of the audience that it was indeed only through organizing themselves that the common people of the world could overcome their difficulties. This had now been proven by the Chinese who had formed new societies which enabled them to grapple with problems that had troubled their society for decades. At this point the meeting was rudely interrupted by the police who objected to the speaker bringing political (*sic*) content into his speech. Two days later the police raided the homes of Tb. Hilman, Ishak, Atmodihardjo, and Djarkasih.

Rukun Asli had now served its purpose. The local PKI leaders decided

---

83   *De Banten Bode*, August 29, 1925.
84   SeeMcVey, Rise, p. 291.
85   See Sartono Kartodirdjo, *Protest Movements in Rural Java* (Kuala Lumpur: Oxford University Press, 1973), pp. 136-40. See also report by Achmad Djajadiningrat, November 11, 1922, 70/2G, Mailr 252x/1923.
86   *De Banten Bode*, September 12, 1925.
87   One of the first issues of *Njala* featured an article on Rukun Asli; see its number of September 11, 1925; see also *De Banten Bode*, September 12, 1925.

that the need for secrecy was no longer important and that Rukun Asli had fulfilled its intention of preparing the ground for the PKI. Soon afterwards, on October 9, 1925, a public meeting was called in Serang to announce the establishment of the Banten section of the PKI.[88] The meeting elected Puradisastra as chairman, Tb. Hilman as secretary and Djarkasih as treasurer of the 37th section of the Indonesian Communist Party. Three commissioners for the party were also elected—H. Alwan, Arman, and Mohammed Ali (Mamak). An office of the PKI was opened in Serang market in a property owned by a Chinese member of the party, Lee Eng Hock. From mid-October nightly meetings were held in the office and also in a local Chinese-owned cinema, the Banten Park.[89] No sooner had the PKI opened its newest section than Banten witnessed its first labor strike when the printing workers on *De Banten Bode* staged a stoppage in a claim for higher wages,[90] Banten's own modest contribution to the strike wave that swept Java in late 1925.[91]

Unfortunately for the Banten PKI, the beginning of the party's activities in the region coincided with growing repression throughout Indonesia as the colonial authorities reacted to the strike wave. Darsono, one of the PKI's main theoreticians, was expelled from Indonesia in September, and the same month Alimin left the country for fear of arrest.[92] Aliarcham and Mardjohan were arrested soon after.

Harassment of PKI meetings was widespread. There was a police presence at all meetings which were frequently closed under one pretext or another. The local administration in Banten took a particularly tough stance towards the PKI, after initially being taken aback by its quick and rapid development.[93] A new government regulation that no person under the age of eighteen could attend political meetings was frequently used by the police to close meetings and arrest speakers, who were held

---

88 *Njala*, October 14, 1925.
89 Ibid., October 21, 1925.
90 *De Banten Bode*, October 24, 31, 1925; *Njala*, October 26, 1925.
91 See McVey, *Rise*, pp. 309-10; *Pemberontakan Nasional Pertama*, pp. 45-46; Poeze, *Tan Malaka*, p. 300.
92 McVey, *Rise*, p. 307. Alimin, like many Indonesian revolutionaries in the 1920s, left Indonesia via Banten, proceeding by boat to the Lampungs and thence being smuggled via Palembang to Malaya. Interview Tje Mamat.
93 See report of Hillen, Governor of West Java, March 8, 1926.

responsible for their being held.[94] Party members in public employ, especially in Serang regency, were dismissed.[95] Even more irksome for the local PKI was the intimidating presence of armed police who would often refuse to allow any who were not party members to enter the meetings. The weekly PKI meeting in Serang on October 22, for example, was attended by three assistant *wedana* (district official) and six policemen, who turned away many peasants because their names did not appear on the PKI membership roll.[96] Two weeks later,a meeting that was to have been addressed by a PKI leader from Surabaya, Go Soei Hoa, was closed because the speaker had not obtained individual permission from the local Dutch Resident.[97] Some days later, on November 8, Puradisastra received a month's imprisonment and Tb. Hilman and Mohammed Ali (Mamak) ten days each for addressing a meeting at which two seventeen-year-olds were present.[98] Permanent police guards were placed on the PKI office in Serang, and the party books seized by the police on the pretext of examining alleged financial irregularities.[99]

Despite its constant difficulties with the police, however, by the end of 1925 the PKI had established itself on a firm basis in Banten. The meetings which the party held every Wednesday in the Banten Park cinema in Serang drew regular crowds of 300, and members were beginning to be recruited in the regencies of Pandeglang and Lebak.[100] A report by Dutch Resident de Vries in late November estimated total PKI membership in the residency at 1,200, and the Resident noted with concern that some religious leaders were being attracted to the party.[101] The PKI leadership evidently viewed their position in Banten with satisfaction, despite the harassment from the authorities. An article in the Batavia PKI daily newspaper, *Njala*, in December noted,

Comrades will understand that Communism has many roads.

94 McVey, *Rise*, p. 292.
95 See *Njala*, November 7, 1925.
96 *De Banten Bode*, November 7, 1925.
97 Ibid., November 14, 1925.
98 *Njala*, November 10, 1925; *De Banten Bode*, November 14, 21, 1925.
99 *De Banten Bode*, November 28, 1925; *Njala*, December 16, 1925.
100 Report of Resident [of Banten] de Vries to Procureur-Generaal, No. 55, November 24, 1925 in Mailr 1245x/25. See also "Bantam Report," pp. 26, 37-38.
101 Ibid. At the same time key recruits were sent by the PKI to Batavia for training.

> Although faced with all the powers of reaction, our membership [in Banten] does not decrease, nor does the political consciousness of our members, but on the contrary it increases like fire igniting a dry field.[102]

But if there was room for some optimism at a local level, at least in Banten, at a national level the fortunes of the PKI were far less happy. The strikes engineered by the party in late 1925 had not only failed to produce any real improvement in the workers' conditions, but they had also seriously undermined the PKI's proletarian base. Key leaders had left the country or been arrested, and in late November the Dutch authorities placed even further restrictions on political meetings.[103] Henceforth all meetings, public or party, required a police presence and five days notice to the authorities. In practice permission was now far more difficult to obtain, the authorities using one subterfuge or another to deny the PKI the right to hold meetings.

These measures only served to confirm the PKI in its intention to stage an armed uprising against the government. As noted earlier, the critical decision was taken at a secret conference of party leaders at Prambanan in Central Java on December 25, 1925.[104] A secret illegal organization, the so-called DO (the Dubbel or Dictatorial Organisatie) was to be established to expedite the task, and the uprising was tentatively fixed for June 18, 1926. Another meeting of the party executive in Batavia on January 13, 1926 decided that any further legal political activity was impossible because of the repressive attitude of the authorities, and all local sections of the party were told to act accordingly by letter on February 1.[105]

102 *Njala*, December 16, 1925.
103 *De Banten Bode*, December 5, 1925.
104 See McVey, *Rise*, pp. 309, 311, 320, 324; Sudijono *Djojoprajitno*, PKI-SIBAR, pp. 6-42; Tamin, *Sedjarah PKI*, pp. 20-21, 49; *Pemberontakan Nasional Pertama*, pp. 50-53. The timing of the rising was fixed for June 18, 1926.
105 McVey, *Rise*, p. 323. Tan Malaka was opposed to the projected uprising, considering it to be "putschist" and doomed to failure. See McVey, *Rise*, pp. 316-322; Poeze, *Tan Malaka*, pp. 307-11; Tamin, *Sedjarah PKI*, pp. 22-25.

The Growth of PKI Support in Banten

Increasing government repression, however, does not seem to have diminished popular support for the PKI in Banten. On the contrary the sense of crisis and of impending rebellion became highly contagious, and the PKI executive in Batavia was to face growing difficulties in keeping the Banten section in check.[106] The Dutch authorities, for their part, tried to keep the contagion under control, but they were clearly not fully aware of how far the "old mole" had undermined confidence in the government.[107]

Although public meetings of the PKI were now virtually forbidden, the party in Banten continued to exist and indeed thrive. Propaganda was spread by means of secret meetings, and elaborate ruses were resorted to in order to avoid police interference. Meetings, for example, were frequently held in woods or PKI members would give *slametan or hajat* (feasts), under cover of which a meeting would take place.[108] In fishing villages meetings would take place at dusk under cover of the men drawing in the nets.[109] In some places local stallkeepers who had joined the PKI allowed their *warung* to be used for informal gatherings.[110] In Serang meetings took place in the Banten Park cinema, as before, but this time under cover of films such as "Jack Dempsey."[111] On other occasions football matches were used as a venue for propaganda,[112] and in Labuan the PKI chairman, Afif, formed an association, Budi Kemulian, ostensibly to promote Arab gambus music but which in fact served the purpose of advancing the revolutionary cause in the Bantenese countryside.[113] Such was the ingenuity of the local PKI that members who found themselves the wrong side of the bars of Serang prison even organized meetings for the other prisoners.[114]

---

106 Interviews with Achmad Bassaif, Tb. Alipan, Afif (Chairman of Labuan PKI in 1926).
107 Interview with Professor G. F. Pijper, Amsterdam, May 27, 1974. In 1926, Professor Pijper worked at the Office of the Adviser for Native and Islamic Affairs. In this capacity he visited Banten on two occasions before the revolt and was frequently told by the Resident, Putman-Cramer, that the PKI in Banten posed no real threat to the colonial authorities.
108 Interviews with Ayot Satriawidjaya, former Secretary of the PKI in Pandeglang, January 1976.
109 Interview with Haji Solichin.
110 *Njala*, January 14, 1926.
111 Ibid., January 29, 1926.
112 *De Banten Bode*, June 12, 1926.
113 Interview with Afif, former Secretary of Labuan PKI.
114 *Njala*, March 1, 1926.

But despite the seemingly endless ingeniousness of PKI propagandists, meetings were sometimes closed by the police and arrests made. In February Tb. Hilman was sentenced to one month's imprisonment for breaking the newly imposed ban on political meetings. In Ciomas fourteen peasants were arrested for holding a secret PKI meeting and sentenced to ten days' imprisonment each.[115] By the end of February twenty-seven PKI members were in detention in Serang prison, including Puradisastra who received a two-month sentence for breaking the ban on meetings.[116] On February 20 thirty-five peasants, all apparently candidate members of the PKI, were arrested in Ciruas for holding an illegal meeting, and two days later a further eighteen peasants of the same district were taken into custody for the same offense.[117]

The local authorities, clearly alarmed by the degree of support for the PKI, tried to cope with the situation by imposing heavier sentences. In March Haji Aliakbar, a PKI propagandist in Serang, received six months' imprisonment, and another local leader in Ciruas, Haji Mardjoek, received four months' imprisonment for breaking the ban on meetings. The chairman of the now defunct "Rukun Asli," Haji Achmad Noer, was also sent to prison for five months.[118] The police, particularly in Serang regency, were reportedly becoming far rougher in their handling of those arrested, and beatings of the detainees were not unknown.[119] But despite the increasing severity of measures taken by the authorities, the PKI's support continued to grow in Banten, a development which apparently caused some surprise even in PKI circles.[120] The Banten correspondent of *Njala* wrote:

The people of Indonesia can see that Banten, the last district where Communism developed, has not been left behind. If we look at the

---

115 *De Banten Bode*, February 20, 1926. The others sent to prison were Haji Mu'min, Abdulmoeti, Nawawi, Kama, Rasidi al Saidi, Haji Oemar, Asmail, Srendawiri, Ahmed, Mad Salah, Asnawi, Alikoesim, Ibrahim, and Alioesoep.

116 Ibid., February 27, 1926; Njala, February 19, 23, 1926. Puradisastra used his trial to denounce the court as "unfit to sit in an abattoir" and said the Governor-General had robbed the Indonesian people of their rights and therefore had no qualifications to pass judgment on Indonesian Communists. See "Optreden tegen eenige leden der Communistische Beweging in Bantam," no. 750 AP, April 24, 1926, Mailr 464x, Vb July 1, 1927 Q10.

117 *Njala*, February 26, 1926.

118 Ibid., March 10, 22, 1926.

119 Ibid., March 4, 1926.

120 Interview with Achmad Bassaif.

development of the movement in our country, there is no one who would have suspected that the political struggle would develop so quickly in Banten.[121]

A measure of how far the struggle had indeed advanced in Banten was the enormous increase in PKI membership. A correspondent of the *Bataviaasch Nieuwsblad*, who visited the region at the end of February 1926, estimated total PKI membership at 12,000 including 500 women members,[122] a figure that was confirmed in March in a report on the Communist movement by the Governor of West Java, W. P. Hillen.[123] This was indeed a dramatic increase in the three-month period since November 1925 when party membership had been estimated at 1,200. But what was the social composition of the party? Even more pertinent, why and how had the PKI been able to grow at such a rapid pace?

Recruitment and Leadership of the Communist Movement

The PKI's astonishing increase in membership came mostly from the peasantry of Banten. With regard to those charged with breaking the ban on meetings, who appeared before the Banten courts in March, the *Banten Bode* reported:

Yesterday morning when this correspondent attended the Serang district court, we were amazed to see that those accused of breaking the ban on meetings were nearly all peasants. They are simple people, illiterate and gullible, of whom it cannot be said that they have any real understanding of Communism. They had been told that if they hesitated to join the party now, they could not join it later and would, therefore, not be exempt from the capitation tax [*hoofdgeld*].[124]

Whether or not the peasants had any "real" grasp of communism, they

---

121 *Njala*, March 1, 1926.
122 *Bataviaasch Nieuwsblad*, February 23, 1926.
123 This estimate was confirmed by Hillen in his report of March 8, 1926. See n. 34.
124 *De Banten Bode*, March 20, 1926.

were clearly attracted by PKI promises that taxation would be abolished for those who joined the movement. Taxation, as the Dutch Resident de Vries recognized in a report on the PKI in Banten in November 1925, was one of the main causes of discontent among the peasants.[125] Because hoofdgeld formed a very large part of the taxes raised in Banten, resentment against it was very marked there. The tax was inflexible, unlike the land tax (*landrente*), and was payable even when harvests were bad. The inflexibility of the hoofdgeld bore particularly heavily on the peasants of Banten, a district where harvests were frequently bad and markedly so in the 1920s. The growth of local taxation and the increasing number of items on which taxes were levied were also important causes of peasant discontent, and were exploited by PKI propagandists. (I will examine the relationship between taxation and the 1926 revolt in detail later.)

But equally important in attracting peasants to support the PKI was the great impression made on them by the PKI as a movement. The Communist Party was far more visible than the Sarekat Islam, and its organization and efficiency had a greater impact on the peasants than the SI at an earlier stage. The presence of far abler leaders than the Sarekat Islam had been able to muster strengthened the impression that the PKI was a movement that was not only here to stay but, indeed, would inevitably take over from the Dutch.[126] The comments on Puradisastra made by Fritz, the editor of the *Banten Bode*, although they are somewhat exaggerated, do nevertheless indicate the reaction of the peasantry towards the PKI leaders:

> Everywhere he [Puradisastra] makes a great impact on the gullible peasants. With his spectacles and briefcase the Bantenese consider him a man of great importance. Peasants and ulama flock to "Rumah No. 13" where they see the bold legend "Office of the Indonesian Communist Party—Banten Section." Inside there are books, files, and newspapers everywhere. PKI "mantri" come and go, naturally with their own spectacles and briefcases, and to the peasants give an impression of a "shadow government." The

---

125 See report of Resident de Vries, November 24, 1925, no. 55 in Mailr 1245x/25.
126 "Bantam Report," p. 50.

arrogance of the Communist officials in the face of the government
has an undeniable effect on the peasants and ulama.[127]

What passed in peasant minds for efficiency and modernity, were important
for developing the PKI's image as a counterforce to the government,
adding strength to the Communist contention that the rebellion could be
successful. The PKI managed to convey the impression not only that the
rebellion would be successful but also that the *pergerakan* (movement)
was strong, inevitable, and irresistible. Even the language and idiom of the
PKI helped to reinforce an image of inevitability and strength. In Banten,
unlike elsewhere, every participant became a PKI member possessing the
mystical red membership card. Leaders were called *promotor* or *pemimpin*.
There were also *kurier* and *mantri* (junior officials). More senior leaders
were appointed *commissaris* (commissioners).

Indeed the PKI structure almost seemed to duplicate that of the central
government at all levels. Such an elaborate structure may have been one
key to the attractiveness of the Communist movement, especially to
elements such as the ulama. The religious leaders were excluded from
the colonial regime by their own alienation from its ethos and because
they did not possess that essential passport, secular education. With
the establishment of an extensive Communist political structure, many
may well have seen an opportunity here to enter the political realm and,
seemingly, to participate eventually in the government that would surely
replace the "infidel" Dutch and their allies, the priyayi.

It did indeed become widely accepted that the end of Dutch authority
was fast approaching and that the PKI would soon take over from the
colonial government. The fact that the Communist movement seemed to
be widespread throughout Indonesia and even to have important allies
abroad only served to reinforce this impression. To a marked extent the
PKI served as an alternative conduit for the expression of the peasant
discontent and protest which had previously found expression in Javanese
traditions of the *Ratu Adil* (Just Prince) and in the Islamic concept of a
holy war (*jihad*).[128]

---

127 *De Banten Bode*, March 6, 1926.
128 G. W. F. Drewes, *Drie Javaansche Goeroes* (Leiden: Vros, 1925), p. 192; "Bantam Report," p. 50.

But if the peasants were clearly the foot soldiers, who were the officers of the movement? In other words, who acted as intermediaries between the small group of Communist artisans and intellectuals whose progress we followed earlier and the peasants as a whole? The number of "conscious" Communists, a term actually used by the rebel leadership itself,[129] was very small and consisted of persons who were largely, though not entirely, artisans,or who had enjoyed some elementary education and/or who had spent some time outside Banten. Men like Bassaif, Tb. Hilman, Ishak, Alipan, Puradisastra, and Djarkasih spring to mind. Alongside these men there was another small group of tradespeople who also acted as influential PKI propagandists.

There was, for example, Haji Santani, a tailor in Cilegon who never lost an opportunity to entreat his customers to join the pergerakan. Some tradesmen were like medieval itinerant journeymen, for example Ibing, a tailor who traveled the whole west coast of Banten, urging people to join the PKI as he went along. Sometimes clerks in local government who joined the PKI managed to retain their positions. Their adherence was particularly useful, for it further convinced the rank and file that the colonial regime itself was infiltrated and therefore ripe to fall. Other benefits flowed from such people: a clerk in the bank in Pandeglang who joined and thereafter saw to it that only PKI members received loans from the bank; Soleiman, a PKI commissaris, was especially useful, for his work as a veterinary officer brought him into contact with a wide range of people, including not only peasants but also cattle dealers and butchers, a notoriously restless group in Banten whose activities were often tied up with the local jawara. Other tradesmen, such as goldsmiths, watchmakers, and stallkeepers, were also enormously helpful to the success of the PKI.[130]

The two groups, however, who figure most prominently as "intermediaries" between the PKI leadership and the peasantry were the ulama and the jawara. Of course, not all ulama and jawara joined the PKI, but significant numbers did, and their involvement was undoubtedly critical to the success of the revolutionary movement in Banten in enlisting

---

129 Ibid., p. 46; interviews with Achmad Bassaif and Ajot Satriawijaya.
130 Interview with Achmad Bassaif.

such large numbers. The PKI took great care to court people it considered of importance and influence in local society precisely because their entry into the movement would be a signal to others of the acceptability, and, indeed, of the desirability of joining too.[131]

The religious leaders in Banten were already alienated from the colonial order, and this divorce of an elite who were paramount in local "civil society" was profoundly destabilizing for the region as a whole. A small number of religious teachers had found a niche in the political order through their appointment as penghulu or religious officials, but this group was not only small, but was also often the target of considerable resentment and hostility. Many, if not most, religious leaders in Banten regarded acceptance of a position with an infidel government as *haram* (forbidden by Islam). Peasants disliked the penghulu because they had to pay them fees on occasions such as marriages. The penghulu were also widely believed to be spies for the local administration, a suspicion that was not without foundation.[132]

For the PKI the resentment of the ulama was grist for their mill. Propagandists never ceased to point out that Islam could not be free under an infidel government, but that communism, which was rule by the people, would mean that religion would be free and not subject to restrictions such as those imposed by the colonial regime. Some PKI leaders, such as Achmad Bassaif and the Sumatran, Hasanuddin, themselves came from a religious background and were skilled in using *dalil* (quotations from the Koran) or *firman* (Allah's commandments) in making their points,[133] thereby gaining easy access to religious leaders.

At virtually all its meetings the PKI made frequent appeals to parallels and precedents in Islamic history to engender among the ulama and the peasants the feeling that the coming revolutionary struggle was not only inevitable but would be victorious because it had God's blessing. Frequent reference was also made to more contemporary struggles, such as that of the Moroccan people under Abd el Krim against infidel Spanish and

---

131 "Bantam Report," p. 41.
132 Pijper, "De Penghulus op Java," pp. 63-96. Interview Kiyai Hassan, Pandeglang, November 18, 1975.
133 Interview Achmad Bassaif. Bassaif, as we have noted, had a Modernist education at the Al-Irsjad school in Batavia but in his propaganda work in Banten he tactfully emphasized his Arabic heritage rather than his education.

French rule.[134] Indeed, even Lenin and the Bolsheviks were portrayed as defenders of Islam and founders of "a state which was just and prosperous and blessed by God [*Negeri yang adil dan makmur dan diridai Allah*] ."[135]

For their part the ulama, regardless of any doubts that they may have entertained about communism and the PKI, were impressed by the Communists' determination and organization, which did indeed seem to lend credence to their arguments that the downfall of the Dutch was at hand. This theme is one that was often advanced in conversations I had in 1976 with several elderly religious leaders who had participated in the 1926 revolt. As one recalled,

> "Some of us understood that communism was really opposed to Islam, but the important thing was that the PKI was the only organization that was willing to fight for independence. This we respected. The Sarekat Islam was as good as dead and only the PKI seemed to offer a path to religious and political freedom."[136]

To most religious leaders the argument of the PKI that it was the successor to the Sarekat Islam was quite convincing, and it is noticeable that, with few exceptions, all those who had previously been active in the Sarekat Islam unhesitatingly went over to the PKI.[137]

To many religious leaders the PKI offered, or seemed to offer, admission to a political realm from which they had been rigidly excluded by the imposition of colonial rule. The troublesome and repressive restrictions the Dutch had placed on religious teaching would be done away with forever. Another informant, also a religious teacher, recalled a PKI leader entreating him to join the party:

> "[Hasanuddin] said that the aim of the PKI was to do away with *perintah* [command, government]. When Indonesia was free there would be no need for taxes, no need for *rodi* [compulsory village-

---

134 Interviews with Achmad Bassaif and Tb. Alipan. See also McVey, *Rise*, p. 315.
135 Interview with Haji Solichin.
136 Interview with Haji Mohammed Tahir, Serang, May 9, 1976. The informant was a former leader of the PKI in Serang in 1926.
137 See "Bantam Report," p. 28.

guard duty], no need to beat the *beduq* [drum to call the faithful to prayers] . Nor would there be any need for the police. All would be felt to be responsibilities. [*Semua akan dirasa kewajiban.*]"[138]

It was indeed enticing for religious leaders to foresee an end of the restrictions imposed by the infidel government, such as the need for religious teachers to obtain a teaching license and keep registers of students.[139] These regulations were seen as a check on their freedom. *Tabligh* (sermons) were always observed by the authorities, especially when they dealt with such sensitive matters as jihad and the struggles of the Prophet Mohammed or of Islamic heroes. In April 1926 the passage of article 153 of the Dutch colonial legal code, under which any statement that was likely to disturb the public order was made punishable by a prison sentence, was skillfully used by the PKI to frighten ulama in Banten into joining the revolutionary movement, although, in fact, the article was not intended to be applied to the utterances of religious teachers.[140]

The relationship between the PKI and those religious leaders who joined the revolutionary movement was to some extent mutually beneficial. For the Communist leadership in Banten the adherence of important ulama meant that the PKI reached a much larger audience than otherwise would have been the case. For the ulama, entry into the PKI seemed to give them a recognition that the colonial government refused to accord. Moreover, it also seemed to reinforce their position in local society and to assure their continued prominence at a time when the advances of the "Great Tradition" seemed to be increasingly eroding the "Little Tradition" of which they were an important part. The PKI offered a chance to redress the balance.

One of the most important religious leaders to join the PKI was Haji Tb. Achmad Chatib, President of the Sarekat Islam in Labuan and son-in-law of Kiyai Haji Asnawi of Caringin, the most influential ulama in Banten at the time. Chatib brought with him an enormous number of his

---

138 Interview with Haji Solichin.
139 Noer, *Modernist Muslim Movement*, pp. 175-76; Pijper, "De Penghulus op Java," p. 77.
140 Interview with Kiyai Haji Abdulhalim, Pandeglang, December 14, 1975. See also Makmun Salim, "Suatu Tindjauan tentang peranan adjaran Islam dalam Pemberontakan 1926 di Banten," *Seminar Sedjarah Nasfonal II* (Yogyakarta, 1970).

followers in the Labuan-Caringin area, including all the former Sarekat Islam members, and his close companion and son of Kiyai Asnawi, Tb. Haji Emed. Haji Emed later recalled to the police their first meeting with Puradisastra, the PKI chairman, in Caringin:

"Puradisastra came to visit us around Djamadi'l-awal 1344 [October 1925]. He praised my brother-in-law for the work he had done in the Sarekat Islam, but said the time of the Sarekat Islam was now past. The aim of the PKI was to obtain the independence of Indonesia. In the struggle to achieve this aim the people of Banten had been left behind. Soon the PKI would take over the government from the Dutch. As I remember,the conversation proceeded as follows:

Puradisastra: What is the basis of the Sarekat Islam?
Chatib: Islam.
P: I too am a Moslem, but I am also chairman of the PKI in Banten.
C: What sort of organization is the PKI?
P: It is a section of the International.
C: What do you mean by International?
P: Well, An International is an organization that makes no distinction of race or religion. Anyone can be a member whether he is Indonesian, Chinese, or European.
C: But what is the purpose of the organization?
P: The granting of mutual help in both worldly and religious matters. Members must consider each other as brothers and comrades.
C: If the protection of religion is one of the aims of the PKI, then I am of accord. Of worldly affairs, however, I have little understanding.
Puradisastra then said that he had no wish to pressure anyone to join the PKI; he only requested help and support."[141]

Whatever other promises the PKI made, and certainly its propagandists were extravagant, it is interesting to note that, unlike Sarekat Islam, it

---

141 Police interrogation report of Haji Tb. Emed, October 23, 1926 in Mailr 786x/1927.

did not claim that it was an Islamic organization, merely that it would respect and protect religion. This comes over strikingly in another interview which the writer recorded with a kiyai who had participated in the revolt. "The Communist movement did not consider religion or race of importance. Everyone was the same, for it was said if we paid attention to race and religion this would weaken our cause and our aims would not be achieved."[142] As the insurrectionary movement gathered momentum, however, this distinction was frequently lost, especially on the rank and file.

The recruitment of Haji Tb. Achmad Chatib and Tb. Emed to the PKI led many other ulama to join, together with their followers.[143] Of all the ulama who participated in the PKI, Chatib had the most political experience as a result of his years in the Sarekat Islam. Moreover, he was a fiery speaker and a man of considerable charisma. Although only thirty years old in 1926,he already had a small madrasah of his own and possessed wide influence because of his position as son-in-law of Kiyai Asnawi. This relationship was widely interpreted in Banten as a sign that the Kiyai of Caringin was at least neutral or even well disposed towards the revolutionaries. The PKI certainly did not seek to disabuse people of this impression.

Other ulama soon followed Haji Chatib's lead. Kiyai Moekri of Labuan together with Kiyai Madoen and Kiyai Tb. Ichyar brought with them a considerable number of their *santri* (students). In Petir, in Serang regency, Kiyai Emed and Kiyai Jahja were recruited to the Communist cause. When Kiyai Abdulhadi of the village of Bangko near Menes joined, he brought with him almost the entire local population.[144]

It was a masterstroke on the part of the Communist leadership to attract these influential ulama to the PKI, for not only did this make it far more likely that large numbers of peasants would join the insurrection, but it also opened up new channels of communication to the Communists at a time when harassment by the authorities was making public agitation impossible. Henceforth,meetings were held in langgar (village prayer houses), mosques, and pesantren, and the santri of the ulama often

---

142 Interview with Kiyai Haji Abdulhalim.
143 Interview with A jot Satriawijaya; see also *Njala*, March 20, 23, 1926.
144 Interview with Haji Afif.

became couriers for the rebels. Several religious leaders, it seems, simply ordered their following to join the PKI. Djarman, a fisherman from Caringin, recalled to the police the following conversation he had with Haji Chatib:

> "In the month of Rowah [March 1926] Haji Chatib approached me several times to join the PKI. One day as I was about to go to Labuan Haji Chatib, who was sitting at the warung of Tb. Emed, called me over and said, Djarman, you must join the PKI soon [*mesti lekas jadi lid kommunis*] because its purpose is to achieve independence [*kemerdekaan*] for all.' I asked Haji Chatib what was meant by this. He replied that after independence all would be freed from taxation. Because Haji Chatib was an influential man in Caringin I trusted him. When I went to Labuan that day I went to see Afif, bought a membership card, and became a Communist."[145]

As Djarman was remarkably frank in his testimony to the police about other matters, there is no reason to doubt his account. Djarman, who was also a former santri of Haji Chatib, entered the PKI in a manner which was not at all unique; indeed it was fairly typical of hundreds of others who followed the lead set by their religious teachers.

Of course, not all ulama joined the PKI. On the contrary,the majority of religious leaders in Banten probably abstained from any direct involvement in the insurrectionary movement, either waiting to see how things developed, or, like Kiyai Asnawi, abjuring entanglement in worldly affairs and confining their hostility to the *kafir* (unbeliever) to the spiritual realm. However, it is remarkable that very few religious leaders in Banten were willing to speak out against the PKI.[146] One of the few who did was Kiyai Jasin of Menes, the only prominent figure of the Sarekat Islam in Banten not to go over to the PKI.[147] Kiyai Jasin did warn people against the incompatibilities between the PKI and Islam but he seems to have found little response. In February 1926 he organized a meeting at Labuan at which Tjokroaminoto himself was the main speaker. But it was perhaps

---

145 Police interrogation report of Djarman, January 4, 1927, Mailr 868x/27, Vb April 13, 1928 06.
146 "Bantam Report," pp. 48-49.
147 Ibid.

an indication of which way the wind was blowing that Puradisastra, who arrived to denounce the veteran Sarekat Islam leader as a lackey of the Dutch, was better received by the crowd.[148] Thereafter Kiyai Jasin took a back seat and made no further forays against the PKI.

The Jawara Element

Second only in importance to the ulama in the revolutionary alliance shaped by the PKI for the uprising in Banten were the jawara, the local men of violence. The jawara often dominated the markets and auctions of the region, and they alone were able to offer effective protection in the countryside. Skilled in martial arts and the use of the *golok* (machete) and *parang* (short sword), they also played an active part in recruiting labor for Batavia and Sumatra. Indeed, it was probably in this latter context that the PKI first came into touch with the jawara, for they were very prominent in Tanjung Priok.

Like the mafioso of nineteenth century Sicily, the jawara of Banten exploited the gaps in communication between the peasant village and the larger society. They thrived on these gaps and reinforced their position by systematic threats and use of violence.[149] The word jawara itself denoted someone who was prepared not only to defy the laws of the land but was also ready to force others to do his will. They are an intriguing local phenomenon and have survived up to the present day. In 1976 I asked a prominent religious personage who had had many dealings with the jawara during the 1945 revolution to define their role for me.

> "Jawara is a Bantenese term for those who are clever in *silat* [kind of fencing, taught also in pesantren in Ban ten] but who also possess other definite skills. Jawara are not synonymous with robbers or thieves, but it is the jawara who are able to guarantee safety and security in the *desa* [village] because people respect them. In general the jawara are very obedient to the ulama. Their spirits find guidance from the ulama. Of course there are those who are

---

148 *Njala*, February 8, 9, 26, 1926.
149 For Sicily, see Blok, *Mafia of a Sicilian Village*, passim.

negative in their conduct, but they can usually be overcome by other jawara."[150]

It is obvious that the jawara would be very attractive to a PKI now firmly committed to a revolutionary course. In sharp contrast to the Sarekat Islam, the PKI, then, actively sought their assistance. In February, the correspondent of *Njala* in Ban ten, "Roodebril" (Puradisastra), noted approvingly the great change that had taken place among the jawara of Banten and how they were now firmly committed to the people's cause.[151] Another prominent PKI member in Banten related to me that Pandeglang prison, which in 1925 had been full, by March 1926 contained only three prisoners. The implication was not that the jawara had radically mended their ways but that their energies had been channeled elsewhere (*"disalurkan ke PKI"*).[152] The success of the PKI in recruiting large numbers of jawara played a vital part in the eventual outbreak of insurrection.

The Spread of Revolutionary Fervor

The entry of both the ulama and jawara into the PKI had an enormous impact on the local peasantry, for the acceptability of the Communist Party to these two "intermediary" groups ensured that large numbers of the peasants also joined the preparations for revolt. The peasants, of course, had their own grievances, particularly, as we shall see, regarding taxes. But the absence of any specific peasant program in the PKI strategy meant that the peasants could only have been won to what was an essentially Jacobin appeal through the mediation of groups such as the ulama and jawara.[153] Their hold and influence on Bantenese society secured a mass base for the revolutionary movement.

Revolutionary fervor was mounting throughout Banten in the first six months of 1926, when evidence of the spread of PKI activity seemed

---

150 Interview with Kiyai Haji Abdulhalim.
151 *Njala*, February 9, 1926; see also "Bantam Report," pp. 23, 29.
152 Interview with Tb. Alipan. Achmad Massaif, who temporarily replaced Puradisastra as the leader of the PKI in Banten, frequently dressed as a jawara himself, clothed in black and carrying a *golok*.
153 On the absence of any specific PKI peasant program, see the critique of Dingley, *Peasants' Movement*, pp. 33-50; McVey, *Rise*, pp. 269, 278, 288.

to appear everywhere. Alarmed by the number of ulama joining the movement, the authorities began to withdraw the teaching licenses from those it was certain were members of the PKI.[154] But many ulama joined secretly, and the PKI itself had now become a largely underground organization. In Serang it was discovered that three prison warders at the local jail had joined the PKI, one of them promising his comrades at a PKI hajat that they need fear no discomfort if they should end up in prison.[155]

Initially, PKI activities were largely centered in Serang regency, the most populous region of Banten, but by March and April 1926 they had spread rapidly into Pandeglang regency and the Rangkasbitung area of Lebak regency. To Dutch observers the situation seemed to be rapidly getting out of hand, a commentator in the *Banten Bode* noting:

> Whole villages, whole districts of our previously quiet region have become restless. A restlessness that has been imported by a small group of arrogant agitators who call themselves Communists. There is almost no village in our region, from which at least one man is not, or has not been, in prison. Men who earlier never came into contact with the law, can now be seen every Monday and Friday sitting in the Serang district court. They have been promised everything and such is their lot in life they have believed it.[156]

Although this observer may have been prone to panic at the spread of Communist influence, it was nevertheless clear that in many Bantenese villages whole populations had gone over to the PKI, and this solidarity provided further proof to members of the invincibility of the revolutionary movement. Much of the solidarity was probably enforced through rigorous boycotts employed in some "desa komonis" against nonmembers,[157] and, particularly in villages where jawara were active, the refusal of assistance and the threat of maltreatment were powerful incentives for joining the

---

154 *De Banten Bode*, April 3, May 1, 1926.
155 Ibid., May 8, 1926.
156 Ibid., March 20, 1926; interview with Haji Solichin, who estimated PKI membership in Banten by June 1926 as in excess of 20,000.
157 "Bantam Report," p. 47.

PKI. In Bangkayung village, Cening subdistrict (Pandeglang regency), peasants who would not join had their trees cut down and they found themselves boycotted at desa feasts.[158] Those who refused to conform ran high risks, in some cases being physically molested. In 1976 Bassaif related:

> "Yes, of course, such things were not so uncommon. You must understand that in 1926 the people of Banten saw for the first time a chance to assert themselves. Nobody was quite sure, even the leaders, how events would develop, but all of us had to work against the deadline of impending revolt. For the first time, too, it seemed as if Banten would not be alone. This was not simply an uprising of peasants led by ulama as in Cilegon [in 1888] . Everyone felt that we were part of a national movement whose chance of success seemed to us reasonable...Solidarity was necessary. Those who were not with us were henchmen of the Dutch [kaki tangan Belanda] ,"[159]

In the villages the spirit of rebelliousness increased throughout 1926. Possession of the red membership card signified that one belonged to the new society and was assured of a place in the new revolutionary order. To some, the membership card assumed a mystical character, possession of it endowing them with properties of invulnerability and invincibility, normally associated with amulets (jimat). To others, it meant more practical things, such as freedom from taxation after the revolt. In some cases the restlessness in the villages manifested itself in a fundamental rejection of the existing order. For example,in villages near Labuan marriages took place without the presence of the penghulu,[160] while in other villages peasants prolonged their fasting and refused to celebrate Lebaran (the feast following Ramadan, the fasting month) on the day stipulated.[161] Officials who investigated villages which were reportedly under PKI influence met with a wall of silence. In Labuan regency, the regent himself, R. A. A. Kartadiningrat, held meetings in villages in the

---

158 De Banten Bode, April 10, 1926.
159 Interview with Achmad Bassaif.
160 De Banten Bode, May 1, 1926.
161 Interview with Haji Gogo Sanjadirdja, Serang, October 27, 1975.

Caringin and Cening areas, and called on the peasants not to support the PKI,[162] but with the PKI now underground the extent of the support for the revolutionary conspiracy remained largely hidden.

In the village of Taktakan, near Serang, which was a PKI stronghold, the local PKI propagandist was said to be endowed with magical powers and if any government official passed the village he would be immediately paralyzed.[163] In some areas large sales of red cloth were reported as peasants made red trousers for themselves to denote their loyalty to the PKI.[164] In another village the peasants refused to elect a new *jaro* (headman). When the wedana of the area visited the village, village elders refused to see him, and he was later abused and addressed contemptuously in low Javanese. One villager told him bluntly: "The government may well need a jaro, but we do not. If we are not afraid of death, why should we be of a jaro."[165]

The unrest in the countryside sometimes showed signs of breaking out in premature violence. In April a policeman was badly beaten up at night in the village of Bojong, near Menes: The same week a Chinese trader in the village of Tanjangdalang, near Caringin, was beaten and robbed.[166] Some weeks later when a Dutchman traveling near Menes was involved in a car accident, he was attacked by a hostile crowd.[167] Elsewhere, Chinese traders and moneylenders were forced to contribute to PKI coffers.[168]

By the end of May 1926 revolutionary expectations were high in Banten. The seeming inability of the government to counteract the growth of the PKI strengthened its members' feeling of invincibility. The alliance forged by the PKI with a considerable number of local ulama and with the jawara, coupled with peasant grievances, were already providing an explosive mixture.

---

162 *De Banten Bode*, June 26, 1926.
163 Ibid., February 27, 1926.
164 "Bantam Report," p. 47.
165 *De Banten Bode*, August 9, 1926.
166 Ibid., May 1, 8, 1926.
167 Ibid., June 12, 1926. The village near which the Dutchman was attacked was a stronghold of the PKI.
168 Ibid., May 8, 29, 1926; interview with Haji Afif. In Cilegon many Chinese traders seem to have contributed to PKI funds.

MAP 1. ADMINISTRATIVE DIVISIONS OF BANTEN IN 1930

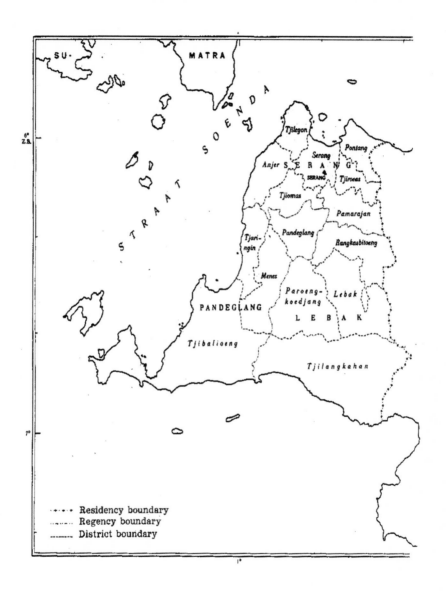

Source: *Volkstelling 1930*, Vol. 1. Native Population in West-Java (Batavia: Landsdrukkerij, 1933). The original spelling has been retained.

CHAPTER TWO
PREPARATIONS FOR INSURRECTION

A lthough the Prambanan conference of the PKI leadership had taken the decision to stage an insurrection in 1926, effective measures to implement this were not taken until the middle of the year, because of the lack of preparedness of the party and the need to develop the illegal organization—the Dubbel Organisasi or "DO." News of the Prambanan decision was communicated to the PKI section in Banten by Sukrawinata, one of the leaders of the Batavia PKI, in early 1926.[1] Sukrawinata met with all the important leaders of the Banten PKI, including Bassaif, Puradisastra, Haji Chatib, Kiyai Moekri, and Entol Enoh.[2] At the same time other participants at the Prambanan meeting traveled around Indonesia informing party sections of the fateful decision.[3]

Such was the state of disorganization among the PKI leadership, however, that, having communicated this historic decision, they left local sections entirely to their own devices regarding its implementation.[4] Sections were instructed to establish their own "DO" and encouraged

---

1   *Pemberontakan Nasional Pertama*, p. 53; interview with Achmad Bassaif.
2   Entol Enoh was a former leader of the Sarekat Islam in Banten. He was jaro (headman) of the village of Tegalwangi, near Menes, for twenty-two years but was dismissed in 1925 after a dispute with the local *wedana*. When he joined the PKI it seems he took the majority of the membership of Sarekat Islam in the district with him. Entol Enoh had a wide influence in the Menes area, comparable with that of Haji Chatib in Labuan. He had close ties with local jawara and would appear to have used them to maintain order in the area. He gave the lead to many other village heads, particularly it seems regarding matters such as tax collection. The circumstances of his dismissal in 1925 as a jaro are not clear, but apparently were related to large sums of overdue taxes for his district which he had tried to discharge in some cases from his own pocket. See letter of Achmad Djajadiningrat, undated, appendix 7, in Vb July 4, 1939-19; see also reports in Mailr 172x/27, Vb July 1, 1927 T10; "Bantam Report," pp. 28, 42, 48.
3   *Pemberontakan Nasional Pertama*, p. 53.
4   Interviews with Achmad Bassaif and Tb. Alipan.

to collect funds for the purchase of arms from abroad. Apart from this, they were to await further orders from the PKI executive. Given the considerable autonomy already granted to local sections in 1925 under the rubric of "federal centralism," it was not a recipe for creating a tight and disciplined revolutionary organization. As the exiled PKI leader Tan Malaka pointed out, it rather had all the makings of a "putschist" adventure.[5]

With local sections of the PKI in Banten and elsewhere already creating the illegal "DO" organization in preparation for the revolt, the leadership of the party was rapidly descending into complete disarray. The trade unions had virtually collapsed after the 1925 strike wave, and between January and April 1926 almost the entire leadership of the PKI left Indonesia, most of them to Singapore.[6] At the same time, the Dutch authorities were clamping down with increasing severity on the party, making any legal activity impossible. In April the PKI daily, *Njala*, instructed all units of the party not to communicate with the executive because of continual police raids on the Batavia headquarters office and interception of the mail.[7] At the end of April the Dutch colonial government delivered the coup de grace to legal PKI activity by adding two new regulations to the legal code, Article 153 bis and ter, which effectively prohibited revolutionary literature and organization.[8] As a result, all party newspapers and journals were forced to close on April 30, and three days later the PKI leadership formally disbanded all units of the party and the Sarekat Rakjat. In May the rump of the PKI leadership in Batavia, faced with police harassment and the whittling away of its local support, decided to move to Bandung.[9]

The authorization to establish illegal underground organizations to prepare for the insurrection seems to have been given to local sections in early 1926. These proceeded largely independent of the PKI leadership, and only in April and May did the latter make some attempt to coordinate

---

5   See his *Massa Actie* (Jakarta: Pustaka Moerba, 1947) [originally published in 1926], passim; see also Poeze, *Tan Malaka*, pp. 313-14; McVey, *Rise*, pp. 316-22.

6   McVey, Rise, p. 474, n. 95.

7   *Njala*, April 6, 1926.

8   Ibid., April 13, 1926; 40 *Tahun* PKI, p. 25; McVey, *Rise*, pp. 326-27; inter-. view with Professor G. F. PijTper.

9   McVey, Rise, pp. 326-28.

and control the local "DO"s. As a result, the problem the PKI faced in some areas was not that of developing a revolutionary potential but rather of keeping local hotheads and militants from taking premature action.[10] This was exemplified in Banten, where the "DO," once set up, was soon thirsting for action.

In Banten a major part of the PKI's appeal had lain precisely in the fact that it seemed an organization geared for action. The "pergerakan" had been formed for a definite purpose, namely the overthrow of the existing order. To a marked extent, therefore, it dovetailed with existing millenarian traditions that had previously found embodiment in Islamic beliefs of the jihad or *perang sabil* (holy war).[11] At a later stage the fervent words, jihad and perang sabil, began to spread among the revolutionary movement in Banten and, increasingly as the revolt approached, victory was to become associated with the establishment of an Islamic state, sometimes even in the form of the restoration of the Sultanate of Banten. This tendency for the planned revolutionary action to become identified with Islamic millenarian traditions was exacerbated by two circumstances. First, almost from the beginning the PKI's development in Banten coincided with plans for the uprising, and second, well before that uprising got under way the majority of the secular leaders of the PKI in Banten were already behind bars.

The early organization of the "DO" in Banten seems to have been entrusted to a committee that consisted of Puradisastra, Tb. Hilman, Bassaif, Haji Chatib, Kiyai Moekri, Entol Enoh, Tb. Alipan, and Soleiman.[12] Two of its members, Entol Enoh and Soleiman, had extensive contacts with Banten jawara, and they used these to good effect in shaping the "DO." One of its first meetings was arranged by Haji Mohammed Arif, the jaro of Dalung, near Serang, who fortunately provided the police with a very full account of the meeting during his interrogation after the revolt.

10 According to Tamin (*Sedjarah* PKI, p. 27), the executive of the PKI in April 1926 consisted of Suprodjo, Kusnogunoko, and Gunawan. The "DO" was set up in April with Suprodjo as chairman. Dutch archival sources also indicate that the "DO" was set up in this period, with Banten as one of its first bases. See "Beknopt Overzicht van de Communistische Ongeregeldheden in Ned. Indi," Vb December 13, 1926 D19.

11 See Sartono, *Peasants' Revolt*, pp. 165, 168-69, 180, 186. In some respects the revolutionary organization, the "DO," seems to have taken the role that tarekat played in earlier revolts in Banten. There is no evidence of any involvement of tarekat in the 1926 revolt.

12 *Pember on takon Nasional Pertama*, p. 60; interviews with Achmad Bassaif, Tb. Alipan.

Arif had been recruited to the PKI in March 1926 by Tb. Hilman,who told him that the purpose of the PKI was to force the government to make concessions to the people over taxation. Later Hilman impressed upon him that he had joined a powerful, awe-inspiring organization whose ultimate aim was to replace the Dutch colonial government.[13] There was no doubt as to the eventual outcome of the struggle, for the PKI had even infiltrated the police and army to ensure victory.

In the month of Silih Sawal (May) Hilman visited Arif and asked him to organize a meeting in Dalung at which many ulama would be present and important decisions would have to be taken regarding the future of the PKI. This Arif proceeded to do:

"I agreed to hold a slametan as a cover for the meeting. Because my house was too,small, the meeting took place at the house of a widow, Nji Arwi, who was in Batavia at the time.

"Before the start of the meeting Arman placed a large red flag with hammer and sickle on the speakers' table. There were more than forty people. Those I remember were Haji Achmad Chatib, Hilman, Hasanuddin, Bassaif, Arman, Soleiman, Ishak, Alirachman, Haji Ayip Achmad, Kiyai Moekri, Kiyai Haji Achmad [of Petir], Haji Adung, Haji Mardjuk, Tje Mamat, Haji Mohammed Ali, and Doeldjawad. Haji Chatib, Hilman, Soleiman, and Hasanuddin sat behind the speakers' table while the rest of us sat on chairs or on the floor.

"The meeting was started by Haji Chatib reciting a prayer in Arabic. After the blessing Hasanuddin spoke. He began by saying that the purpose of the meeting was to discuss further the organization of the DO. For this purpose it was essential that as many jawara [golongan jawara] as possible join, for only they were brave enough to meet the demands the PKI would make of them. He went on, 'We must choose those who are brave enough to guarantee the safety of the PKI so that if a member of the party is ill-treated by the police then that policeman will be killed by the DO. The DO will also have to look for money by any means

---

13   Police interrogation report of Haji Mohammed Arif, October 25, 1926, in Mailr 67x/1927, Vb April 13, 1928 06.

available including theft.' Soleiman then followed Hasanuddin, stressing the importance of developing the DO and of collecting money for the purchase of arms.

"Haji Chatib spoke next, beginning by explaining the hadith Djichnad which showed that the Prophet Mohammed when he advanced the cause of Islam faced all manner of difficulties but he did not shrink from the use of war to propagate Islam. 'Therefore,' he continued, 'my hope is that we all defend the PKI by any means possible.' Then he explained the meaning of the perang sabil which was to be waged against all non-Moslem peoples. He ended by saying that, just as 'unclean cloth had to be cleaned with soap, so an impure world had to be cleansed with blood [*karena kain kotor mesti dibersihkan dengan sabun, demi dunia yang kotor mesti dibersihkan dengan darah*].'

"Towards the end of his speech I remember Haji Ayip Achmad intervened to say that Ishak [the printer on the *Banten Bode*] was unfit to be a leader as he was not a true Moslem and therefore unacceptable. Haji Chatib rose angrily to his feet and said, 'I am not afraid of being hanged or of being exiled for defending Communists. All who are have no place in the PKI.'

"The meeting then proceeded to discuss finances. Haji Chatib was angry to learn that there was very little money in the coffers of the PKI in Serang, 'In Labuan,' he said, 'the PKI has already collected more than 2,000 guilders. We are ready to wage war on the government. I have had enough of [*saya sakit hati kepada*] the government because the people are crushed by taxes. If this continues the people will die from hunger. For me it is better to die in war than from starvation.'

"Hasanuddin then spoke again and said that Haji Chatib was correct in saying that it was vital now that as much money be collected as possible for the coming struggle. Funds were needed to buy arms and to pay for the expenses of propagandists and couriers. Then with his right hand Hasanuddin pointed to his stomach, and continued by saying, 'If my stomach is fat, then my hand will be too. It is the hand that passes the food to the stomach just as it is the priyayi who support the *raja* [ruler] . If the ruler is rich, then so are the priyayi. But we must remember that the wealth of the ruler and the priyayi are derived from the people. Because of that all rulers must be killed by the PKI.' After Hasanuddin finished everybody applauded loudly and threw their hats into the air. Then Haji Achmad of Pancur spoke to close the meeting, 'We must remember, brothers, not to be too hasty. This is not an easy business. Remember the hadiths we have learned. We must be fully prepared for a jihad. Hasty work is Satan's temptation. Slow but sure work is God's desire.'"[14]

The meeting concluded by electing a new executive for the Banten PKI. In part this was prompted by the departure from Banten of Puradisastra and of Achmad Bassaif, who was to continue as a linkman between the Batavia PKI and Banten, and partly because of the need to accommodate the new "DO." In future there was to be an executive of the PKI and a separate executive for the "DO." As President of the PKI Banten section the meeting elected Ishak, with Haji Mohammed Nur as secretary and Arman as treasurer. For the executive of the new "DO," which was also called the "golongan jawara," Hasanuddin was appointed president, with Solei-man as vice-president. Two commissioners of the "DO" were also selected, Tb. Hilman and Alirachman. In addition, Haji Achmad Chatib was given leadership of the "golongan ulama" (religious section) with the title "Presiden Agama PKI Sectie Banten" (Religious President).[15]

In practice, of the two new executives, that of the "DO" was increasingly to become the more important, as any legal activity by the PKI was now impossible. In the weeks and months after the May meeting in Dalung, however, even the "DO" executive was to face difficulties as more and more leaders of the Banten PKI were taken into police custody. As we shall see, this allowed leadership of the revolutionary movement to fall into the hands of an ad hoc committee led by Haji Achmad Chatib which was composed almost entirely of ulama.

Already before the May meeting, the PKI in Banten had begun collecting money for the purchase of arms from its membership. An extensive network of contacts was established for this purpose which seems

---

14   Ibid.
15   Ibid.

to have been particularly effective in Serang and Pandeglang regencies. Tb. Haji Emed was appointed treasurer of the DO in Pandeglang regency and proved an efficient and capable administrator of the finances of the revolutionary organization. Undoubtedly Tb. Emed's prestige as the son of Kiyai Asnawi of Caringin greatly assisted the PKI in its fundraising activities. Often the collection of monies for arms was accompanied by the spread of fantastic rumors regarding the coming revolt. In the police interrogation of Djar-man, the fisherman in Caringin, he later told them that he had collected money for the purchase of arms because Haji Chatib had told him that Japan was ready to assist with the forthcoming revolt.[16] Others gave because they were told that the money was to pay for the transportation of soldiers from Soviet Russia who would arrive in the bay of Banten in a giant fleet.[17] In the village of Ciomas, Serang regency, the local PKI leader, a peasant called Martadjani, proclaimed that those who did not contribute would not be considered as true Moslems by the Sultan of Banten after the revolt and would have their property confiscated.[18] In a neighboring village to Ciomas, Barugbug, H. Mu'min, a PKI propagandist, said that all who did not contribute to the revolutionary coffers would be robbed and killed after the revolt.[19]

Such rumors of aid from overseas and also intimidation were clearly partly responsible for the monies that began flowing into the PKI coffers. But there is also little doubt that in many cases peasants gave freely, sometimes even going to the length of pawning coconut trees, land, buffalo, or the money they had saved to make the pilgrimage to Mecca.[20] The fact that they gave so generously and in such large numbers indicates the growing millenarian atmosphere that accompanied the preparations for revolt. This atmosphere was largely the PKI's creation, as its organization and efficiency left the peasants impressed if not awe-struck. Members of the "DO," which both in the popular mind and in practice became

16 Police interrogation report of Djarman, October 6, 1926, Mailr 67x/1927, Vb April 13, 1928 06. Djarman was instructed by Tb. Emed to collect f120 from each party member. The sum could be paid in installments of 12 cents per month for ten months. Elsewhere PKI collectors instituted a sliding scale of payments of contributions for the revolt according to the means of the party member.
17 *De Banten Bode*, June 5, 1926.
18 Report of Resident of Banten, Putman-Cramer, August 29, 1927, in Mailr 523x/27.
19 Ibid.
20 Interviews with Tb. Alipan and Achmad Rasyidi, Serang, February 18, 1976.

indistinguishable from the PKI, were to be regarded as soldiers of the party. Villages where the PKI commanded overwhelming support either developed a counter administration with PKI-appointed "civil officials" and "military officials" (*penghubung militair or penghubung desa*), or the existing village administration with the jaro at its apex went over to the PKI.[21] As this new "administration" promised to abolish taxation, to institute an Islamic state, and even to provide free cigarettes and train rides, it is understandable why the peasants were so willing to contribute to the organization, which also had the support of many influential ulama and jawara.[22]

But if preparations for insurrection were proceeding apace in Banten, the local leaders found to their consternation that developments elsewhere left much to be desired. In May, after the meeting to establish the "DO" in Dalung, Haji Chatib and Hasanuddin left Banten for Bandung where the PKI executive had recently moved from Batavia. The two leaders went to discuss the purchase of arms and the coordination of the various sections of the PKI for the planned insurrection. They discovered, however, that the leadership in Bandung had done nothing to implement the Prambanan decision of December 1925 and were even unable to help with the arms shipments. Hermawan, a leader of the PKI in the Priangan, told Haji Chatib and Hasanuddin that there was considerable dissension among the PKI leadership regarding the planned revolt. There was no chance of an uprising in June or for some months to come, as the illegal "DO" was insufficiently developed. Hermawan told the two Bantenese leaders that confidence in the PKI executive among many local sections was minimal because of the indecisiveness at the top. The Priangan leader concluded by advising Haji Chatib and Hasanuddin that every section must make its own preparations for the revolt.[23]

Dismayed by their reception, Haji Chatib and Hasanuddin returned to Banten to decide on their next step. Hasanuddin now apparently tried to procure arms from Malaya through PKI-contacts in West Sumatra. Little seems to have come of this, but it did unfortunately attract the attention

---

21 "Bantam Report," pp. 42-43.
22 Ibid.
23 Report of Resident of East Priangan to Hillen, Governor of West Java, December 21, 1926, no 486/zg, Vb July 1, 1927 T10; interview with Achmad Bassaif.

of the Dutch authorities. On May 19 the recently appointed Resident of Banten, F. C. Putman-Cramer, informed the Regent of Pandeglang, R. A. A. Kartadiningrat, that intelligence reports from Medan indicated that weapons were to be sent from Sumatra to Java via Labuan and that the family of Kiyai Asnawi was involved.[24] Kartadiningrat replied to Putman-Cramer by arguing that there was no evidence of the involvement of Kiyai Asnawi of Caringin in the PKI or of his son-in-law, Haji Chatib.[25] Kiyai Asnawi had personally assured him that no one in his family was a member of the PKI. Kartadiningrat was prepared to accept this assurance, as the kiyai had abstained from involvement in worldly affairs for many years and had refused to join or approve of the Sarekat Islam. Indeed the only danger Kartadiningrat feared from the family of the kiyai was if they were plagued by police spies or agents provocateurs.[26]

Protected from immediate arrest by the assurances of the regent, Haji Chatib continued energetically to raise support for the coming revolt. Meetings of the rebels now took place in mosques or langgar to avoid police spies, or at night in woods with jawara posted to look out for spies. The rebel leaders, thwarted in their attempts to procure arms through Bandung (the PKI headquarters), now looked to assistance from Batavia. The PKI leadership in the capital was, like that in Banten, firmly committed to the Prambanan decision to stage an armed revolt and was also growing increasingly impatient with the executive's postponement of action. In late May a meeting of the "DO" executive in Banten took place in Caringin. Those present at the meeting, who included Haji Chatib, Tb. Emed, Hasanuddin, and Afif, the chairman of the PKI in Labuan, decided that the Banten PKI should coordinate its actions more closely with the Batavia section. The revolt should proceed as soon as possible, one suggested date being August 31, the birthday of the Dutch Queen Wilhelmina.[27] Afif and Hasanuddin were dispatched to Batavia to meet with PKI leaders there. They took with them 250 guilders to buy arms from Djojpranoto, a PKI leader who Bassaif had promised could obtain

---

24 Hillen to Governor-General, unnumbered, November 26, 1926, Mailr 1181x/26, Vb July 1, 1927 S10.

25 Ibid. It was fortunate for Haji Chatib that he had joined the PKI after it had gone underground.

26 Ibid.

27 Interview with Afif. Statement of Djarman to the police, October 6, 1926, Mailr 67x/1927, Vb April 13, 1928 06.

guns. The Batavia meeting was evidently more promising than the earlier trip to Bandung, for in early June Afif and Hasanuddin returned to Batavia with a further 1,865 guilders for the purchase of arms.[28]

In the meantime, senior PKI leaders had met in Singapore in April and had decided to proceed with the implementation of the Prambanan decision. Alimin and Musso were dispatched to Moscow to secure the approval of the Comintern for the revolt while the other PKI leaders— Sardjono, the chairman, Budisutjitro, Winanta, and Sutan Said Ali— returned to Java to prepare the party for the revolt.[29] On their return after several months' absence the PKI leaders were alarmed to discover that, while some sections were ready for immediate action and were growing impatient with what they regarded as indecisive leadership, other sections were unprepared for revolt or were even opposed to the idea.

To try and bring some coordination and leadership to the party, Sardjono, the PKI chairman, called a meeting to discuss the Prambanan decision in Bandung in late June. Prior to this he hurried to Banten to meet with local PKI leaders. In Caringin he met with Haji Chatib, Tb. Emed, Soleiman, Hasanuddin, Tb. Hilman, Ishak, and Sardjono. The PKI chairman appears to have visited Banten with two purposes in mind. First, Sardjono was concerned to prevent any precipitate action by the Banten PKI and seems to have assured the Bantenese that the PKI leadership was determined to implement the Prambanan decision. Second, he went to raise more money for the PKI. Here too he was not to be disappointed, and he returned to Bandung with a further 1,000 guilders raised from the Banten PKI.[30]

Because of Sardjono's trip to Banten, the Bandung meeting was delayed, and it did not finally begin until June 22. It took place in a pondok in a rice field at Andir, on the outskirts of the city. Thirteen PKI leaders were present, including Sardjono, Budisutjitro, the PKI secretary-general, Kusnogunoko from Batavia, Marsudi from Surabaya, Djamaluddin

28   Ibid.; statement of Tb. Emed to the police, September 13, 1926, Mailr 868x/ 27, Vb April 13, 1928 06.

29   *Pemberontakan Nasional Pertama*, p. 54; see also "The Governor-General's Report of 1927" in McVey and Benda, *Communist Uprisings*, p. 8.

30   Statement of Djarman of October 6, see n. 195. Banten seems to have been one of the chief sources of funds for PKI arms purchases. See also "testimony" of Ongko D, in Djojoprajitno, PKI-SI BAR, p. 65; Tamin, *Sedjarah* PKI, p. 30.

Tamin from West Sumatra, Magas from South Sumatra, and Gunawan, also from Batavia. The conference lasted for four days until June 26 and, despite the fact that of the PKI's thirty-seven sections only four—Banten, Batavia, Priangan, and South Sumatra—pronounced themselves ready for revolutionary action, Sardjono managed to persuade the other delegates present that there was no future for the PKI except by resorting; to armed revolt.[31]

The Arrest of the Serang PKI Leaders

Sardjono's visit to Caringin in June and the outcome of the Bandung conference seem to have convinced the Banten PKI leaders, at least temporarily, of the necessity of coordinating any revolutionary activity in Banten with action elsewhere. In July, when Djojopranto of the Batavia PKI visited Caringin to request money from Haji Chatib and Tb. Emed, he was met with a frosty reception and the reply that the Banten PKI now recognized the PKI executive (*hoofdbestuur*) in Bandung as the sole source of authority in the party.[32] A similar reply awaited two PKI delegates from Buitenzorg (Bogor), Mochtar and Haji Sinting, who visited Haji Chatib in the first few days of August and apparently asked him to consider launching an insurrection on August 31. Haji Chatib refused, pleading that while the Banten section of the PKI were ready and willing to participate in the coming revolt, they would loyally await instructions from the Bandung executive before taking such action.[33]

However, Haji Chatib and the Banten PKI's trust in and loyalty to the PKI executive under Sardjono in Bandung was to be shaken by events in August. Throughout 1925 and 1926, as the PKI drifted inexorably towards armed revolt, the movement found itself increasingly weakened by the removal of key leaders through arrest or exile. This process was also at work at a local level in Banten. Already in May Puradisastra left Banten for Garut in order to evade arrest. At the same time Achmad

---

31 Tamin, *Sedjarah* PKI, pp. 30, 49; McVey, Rise, pp. 328-29, 481 n. 31. See also "Beknopt Overzicht van de Communistische Ongeregeldheden," Vb December 13, 1926 D19.
32 Interview with Haji Afif.
33 Ibid.; statement to the police of Djarman, October 6, 1926, Mailr 67x/1927, Vb April 13, 1928 06.

Bassaif also left Banten and became preoccupied with the preparations for revolt in Batavia. At the beginning of July, Hasanuddin, who had replaced Puradisastra and Bassaif as. the effective leader of the PKI in Banten, was arrested by the police in Batavia.[34] The loss of these three leaders was only the prelude to a more disastrous series of arrests in August.

Throughout the month of July tension had been mounting in Banten. Peasants in many areas who had joined the PKI eagerly awaited the anticipated day of retribution, when all Dutchmen and servants of the "infidel" government were to be killed. The leadership of the revolutionary movement found it increasingly difficult to keep a grip on events. Zealous propagandists had recruited peasants to the PKI with the promise that the revolt would not be long in coming.[35] Delay ran the risk that either this support would be dissipated or the revolutionary movement would be weakened through arrests or premature moves by the rebels.

The tension was further fueled by rumors which seemed to indicate that the day of revolt was fast approaching. Foreign troops were widely expected to arrive from Soviet Russia or from Turkey. A pronouncement by Kiyai Asnawi of Caringin that prospective pilgrims should not undertake the haj to Mecca in 1926 because of the uncertain political situation in Arabia, was widely interpreted as a sign from the kiyai that Bantenese should remain at home to witness a great event.[36] The mounting unrest gave rise in some villages to fasting by the rebels and to several incidents of violence. On July 16 roadblocks were instituted near the village of Kadu-hejo (Menes) and several days later a wealthy haji and moneylender was robbed and shot dead in Petir.[37] The authorities began to receive alarming reports of fasting and the purchase of white cloth that were said to signal the imminence of a general uprising in Banten. [38] Even more alarming was a report received from the police in Semarang who had intercepted a letter between two PKI leaders in the city indicating that Kiyai Asnawi

---

34   De *Banten* Bode, July 10, 1926.
35   Interviews with Achmad Bassaif, Afif and Achmad Rasyidi, and Ajot Satria-wijaya.
36   Letter of W. P. Hillen, Governor of West Java, to Governor-General de Graeff, December 31, 1926, G5/48/3 Mailr 868x/ Vb April 13, 1928 06.
37   *De Banten Bode*, July 17, 24, 31, 1926.
38   "Verhoogde Communistische Actie in het Bantamsche," Report of Governor of West Java Hillen, to Governor-General Fock, August 16, 1926, G/5/25/17, Mailr 808x/ 26, Vb July 1, 1927 Q10; see also Blumberger, *Communistische*, p. 59; Soerabaaisch *Courant*, August 21, 1926.

would support the PKI in any uprising against the Dutch.[39]

The reports caused sufficient concern to the Dutch authorities for them to decide that preventive action was urgently needed. On August 13 the police raided the house in Serang of a PKI member called Michnar and uncovered plans for fomenting unrest, including the sabotage of the railway lines between Batavia and Banten. The Resident, Putman-Cramer, requested additional assistance from the authorities in Batavia and on August 15 police reinforcements arrived. The following day a company of Menadonese troops was sent to Banten under the command of Captain Becking to carry out military exercises.[40]

In the days after the raid on Michnar's house most of the leaders of the PKI in Serang regency were arrested. First among them were Soleiman, Atmodihardjo, and Alirachman, who were holding a meeting at Michnar's house at the time of the raid. To the alarm of the authorities an officer of the Fieldpolice, Mohammed Saleh, was also present and was found to be involved in the PKI. They were soon followed into custody by other leading members of the Serang PKI, including Djarkasih, the cycleshop owner, Haji Ayip Achmad, "the jago of Serang," Arman, and Haji Mohammed Nur, the former chairman of Rukun Asli and secretary of the "DO." Several arms caches were also discovered by the police. In the village of Dalung, where the headman, Haji Mohammed Arif, was a member of the PKI, six revolvers were found hidden in a well. In the village of Ciruas, also in Serang regency and likewise a PKI stronghold, 800 golok were discovered that had been forged especially for the forthcoming revolt. In the villages of Pabuaran, Pancur, and Gunungsari, all in Serang regency, Mauser pistols, Beaumont rifles, and considerable quantities of white clothing were unearthed in police searches. The police also discovered that some 10,000 guilders had been reportedly collected in Banten for the purchase of arms and the funding of the revolt. [41]

---

39 Report of Hillen to Governor-General, December 31, 1926, G5/48/3, Mailr 868x/27, Vb April 13, 1928 06.

40 Interview with M. Padmadisastra, Rangkasbitung, December 23, 1975; the informant was a mantri-politie in Serang in August 1926. See also *Bataviaasch Nieuws-blad*, August 17, 1926; *De Banten Bode*, August 21, 28, September 4, 1926.

41 *Algemeen Indische Dagblad*, August 17, 1926; *Nieuwe Soerabaaische Courant*, September 1, 1926; "Verklaring Mas Wiria di Koesoema," *De Landsdienaar*, 3, 9, September 1927, pp. 459-61. The arrests apparently took place as a result of the PKI being infiltrated by another agent of the field-police, Harunadjaja. The latter was murdered in 1946. Interview with Haji Solichin, Serang,

The wave of arrests and the seizure of rebel arms supplies left the PKI in Banten severely exposed and weakened. This was particularly the case in Serang regency. Two key leaders who escaped the first police dragnet, Tb. Hilman and Ishak, were arrested in September,[42] Tb. Hilman having been tracked down by the turncoat Raden Oesadiningrat, who was now in the service of the police in Banten. Puradisastra, "the father of Bantenese communism," was arrested by the police in Garut and brought back to Serang for questioning.[43] By the end of September some 200 arrests had been made, nearly all of them in Serang regency although arrests were also taking place elsewhere in Banten now. In Rangkasbitung, in Lebak regency, the four main leaders of the local PKI—Tjondroseputro, Atjim, Salihun, and Tju Tong Hin—were arrested in late September.[44]

For their part the Dutch authorities were confident by the middle of September 1926 that they had averted a serious threat of revolt in Banten through the timely arrest of nearly all the known PKI leaders in the area. The troops who had been sent to Banten in August were withdrawn in September, after having carried out military exercises in the Serang regency.[45] Clearly the PKI in Banten had suffered a critical reverse. Of the leaders elected to executive positions in the PKI and the "DO" at the meeting in Dalung in May, all were in police custody by the end of September, with the exception of Haji Achmad Chatib. Those arrested included all of the original band of Communists who had established the Banten PKI a year earlier in August and September 1925. Of that group only Bassaif remained at large, feverishly making plans for the insurrection in Batavia. Thus what might be termed the "secular Communists" were now all behind the bars of Serang prison. The leadership of the PKI was now left entirely in the hands of ulama and jawara and it was they who were to lead the peasants in revolt in November.

March 6, 1976; *De Banten Bode,* September 4, 1926.

42 *De Banten Bode,* September 25, 1926.

43 *Java Bode,* September 18, 1926; De Banten Bode, September 18, 1926.

44 *De Banten Bode,* September 25, 1926.

45 See report of Governor of West Java Hillen, to Governor-General, September 8, 1926, G 5/27/19, Mailr 1059x/Vb July 1, 1927 S10; report of Hillen to Governor-General, October 26, 1926, G/5/33/18, Mailr 1059x/26, Vb July 1, 1927 S10. See also report of Gobée, Adviser for Native and Islamic Affairs, "Politieke Toestand in het Gewest Bantam," H60 October 29, 1926, Mailr 1053x/26, Vb July 1, 1927 S10.

The Eve of the Revolt

Although the PKI executive at its meeting in Bandung in June had decided to proceed with plans for an armed revolt, the party leadership still remained hesitant. It still faced difficulties in controlling local sections many of whom, like Tegal, were in favor of immediate insurrection. The Banten PKI which had supported Sardjono and the executive in June was by August becoming sharply critical of the lack of leadership from Bandung.[46] At the end of July one of the executive leaders who favored revolt, Winanta, was detained by the police in Bandung.[47] Many of the remaining leaders, such as Subakat, Suprodjo, Kusnogunoko, and Djamaluddin Tamin, were beset by doubts and were increasingly won over to the position of Tan Malaka who, from his exile in the Philippines and Singapore, had delivered a trenchant critique of the PKI's planned revolt.[48] The militant local sections led by Tegal and Pekalongan used the replacement of Governor-General Fock by the reportedly more liberal A. C. De Graeff, to press for an immediate revolt. On August 22, in a now rather desperate attempt to control the situation, the executive sent representatives to local sections to consult on the proposed revolutionary action. They were warned not to go over to immediate revolutionary action and told that "federative centralism" was to be replaced by democratic centralism in strict Leninist fashion.[49]

These belated moves on the part of the PKI executive, however, were doomed to failure. In August three sections in Central Java refused to support postponement of revolutionary action any longer.[50] The PKI leader in Ceribon, Abdulmuntalib, sought support for this position in Banten, where he was received by Haji Chatib. Haji Chatib's arguments against revolt when he had met with Sardjono in June had receded, and he now favored revolt at the earliest possible date. Indeed the Banten PKI had seen its strength seriously dissipated as a result of the wave of arrests in August. To delay any longer could risk the total collapse of the PKI in Banten.

---

46 Interview with Achmad Bassaif.
47 McVey, *Rise*, pp. 329, 481 n. 31; Poeze, *Tan Malaka*, p. 318.
48 Poeze, *Tan Malaka*, pp. 317-22.
49 Ibid., p. 323; McVey, Rise, p. 330; interview with Achmad Bassaif.
50 Poeze, *Tan Malaka*, p. 325; McVey, Rise, pp. 331-33, 340.

At the beginning of September Bassaif and Sukrawinata, the vice-chairman of the Batavia PKI, held further discussions with Haji Chatib, Kiyai Moekri, Tb. Haji Emed, and Afif in Caringin. It was agreed that the Banten PKI would support the initiative of the Batavia section in forming a committee to coordinate the insurrection.[51] Afif followed Bassaif and Sukrawinata back to Batavia a few days later with the news that the situation was deteriorating in Banten and the number of arrests was increasing daily. It was feared that Haji Chatib and other leaders in Labuan and Menes would soon follow the Serang PKI leaders into detention. Meeting with the Batavia PKI leaders in the Hotel Borneo in Weltevreden Afif promised the support of the Banten PKI in the revolt but pleaded that there should be no further delays. The revolutionaries in Banten could still muster substantial mass support particularly in Pandeglang regency, but to wait much longer might prove fatal.[52]

Soon after Afif's departure from Batavia, the leaders of the PKI in the capital set up a committee to coordinate the insurrection. The committee, formed on September 13 and called the Komite Pemberontak (Insurrectionary Committee) or the Komite Penggalang Republik Indonesia (Committee of Support for the Indonesian Republic), sent out messengers to all sections to obtain recognition as the organizing committee in preparing the revolt. Despite the fact that only five sections were willing to do this—Padang, Tegal, Priangan, Batavia, and Banten—the committee proceeded in its intention and fixed the day of the revolt for November 12.[53]

As the day of the revolt approached the rebels in Banten began to make feverish last-minute preparations despite further debilitating arrests and some desertions from the revolutionary cause, ironically often among those who had been longest in the PKI.[54] Returning from his meeting in

---

51 Interviews with Achmad Bassaif and Haji Afif.

52 Ibid.

53 McVey, *Rise*, pp. 340-44; Poeze, *Tan Malaka*, p. 327; Pemberontakan *Nasional Pertama*, p. 53; interview with Achmad Bassaif, who is the unidentified person in the photograph on p. 52 of *Pemberontakan*. The members of the Komite included Sukrawinata, Baharuddin Saleh, Mahmud Sitjin alias Mohammed Jusuf, Samudro, Hamid Sutan, and Herojuwono.

54 A number of PKI members went underground in Batavia or fled to Sumatra. In some cases they left the PKI altogether, while in others they left Banten sometimes fearing their own ability to control the rebel movement there. Interview with Achmad Rifai, Chairman of the PKI subsection in Pandeglang in 1926. Others who fled included Mohammed Ali (Mamak), an

Batavia with PKI leaders, Afif was startled to see at Tanah Abang railway station, a police officer from Menes, Mangoendikaria. Realizing he was probably being followed, he became anxious about communicating the results of the Batavia meeting to Haji Chatib:

> "I got back to my house at 2 p.m. My wife had food prepared but I couldn't eat a thing because I was too nervous. About 2.30 the Assistant Wedana (Mas Wiriadikusumah) called. We had known each other since school days. He warned me that the Veldpolitie from Pandeglang would probably arrest me that day. After he left I hurriedly wrote a note to Haji Chatib and destroyed some papers I did not want to fall into police hands. About 4 p.m. the police arrived and I was taken to Pandeglang for questioning."[55]

Unluckily for Afif he was less circumspect about disposing of ammunition he had hidden in his house, and the police became interested again in the underground PKI.

The arrest of Afif, who was the PKI chairman in Labuan, was prompted by the renewed attention of the Fieldpolice (Veldpolitie) to PKI activities in Pandeglang regency. The Veldpolitie, unlike the local administrative police, were commanded by Dutch officers and were directly responsible to the Dutch Resident and not to the regents. They were a well-armed motorized force that in the politically charged atmosphere of the 1920s spent much of their time in checking the activities of the Sarekat Islam and the PKI. Frequently, it seems, they aroused the resentment of regents because of what was seen as their encroachment on one of the traditional preserves of Java's priyayi, maintenance of law and order in native society. This is amply illustrated in the dispute which developed between the Regent of Pandeglang, R. A. A. Kartadiningrat, and the Resident of Banten, F. C. Putman-Cramer, over the danger posed by the PKI in Banten.

On September 6 at a monthly *serba* (meeting of the Resident with the three local regents), Putman-Cramer told Kartadiningrat that the

---

important Bantenese Communist in the revolution of 1945.

55   Interview with Afif.

Veldpolitie had received intelligence reports of increased PKI activity in Pandeglang regency including fas-ing (*pati geni*) and the purchase of white cloth. Kartadiningrat replied that he had instructed his subordinates to keep a strict watch for such activities, but he himself felt that there was a chance that the PKI threat was being magnified.[56] In Kartadiningrat' s view too many arrests were taking place, and it was this and the activities of police spies that were fueling social discontent in Banten and not the PKI. The frequent appearance of the heavily armed Veldpolitie on their motor-bikes in the countryside was having a disturbing effect on the peasants. Two days after the meeting when Afif was arrested in Labuan, Kartadiningrat judged this action of the Veldpolitie to be unnecessary despite the discovery of ammunition in Afif's home.[57]

The ill feeling that developed between the Regent of Pandeglang and the Dutch Resident of Banten undoubtedly protected the underground PKI, and it was notable that when revolt broke out in November 1926, resistance was concentrated in the Pandeglang regency. On September 13th, for example, Kartadiningrat received a report from the Wedana of Pandeglang of unrest in the village of Cadasari. Fasting was alleged to have taken place, and a local kiyai, Haji Soegiri, was said to have imposed a levy on villagers for the purchase of arms. Kartadiningrat himself questioned Haji Soegiri about the reports and, when the kiyai steadfastly denied the allegations, decided that there was no need to send him to Serang for further questioning by the Veldpolitie there. As was to become evident later, the regent gravely underestimated the strength of the PKI. To a warning from the ill-fated Wedana of Menes about the deteriorating situation in his area, Kartadiningrat was reported to have replied scornfully, "You are as frightened as a woman."[58]

Kartadiningrat did not hide from visiting Dutch officials who he felt might be sympathetic, his views with regard to the Resident and what he saw as the undermining of his own authority by the activities of the Veldpolitie. In September when G. F. Pijper, an official of the Office

---

56   Report of Hillen to Governor-General, unnumbered, November 26, 1926, Mailr 1181x, Vb July 1, 1927 S10.

57   Ibid.

58   Report of Hillen to Governor-General, no G 13/9/12, December 29, 1926, Mailr 172x/27 Vb July 1, 1927 T10.

for Native and Islamic Affairs, visited Banten to meet local ulama, he was surprised to hear Kartadiningrat be so free and outspoken about Putman-Cramer and Lucardie, the Commander of the Veldpolitie in Banten. Two weeks later Pijper received a letter from the regent in which he complained bitterly of the "latest outrage of the Veldpolitie."[59] In his letter Kartadiningrat recounted the arrest by the Veldpolitie of Ishak, the Communist printer on *De Banten Bode*, on the *pendopo* (front verandah) of the kabupaten in Pandeglang without the regent even being informed. Clearly, the incident revealed again that the Resident and the police officers directly responsible were singularly lacking at times in the respect that a man like Kartadiningrat felt that he deserved. Yet at the same time the incident illustrates strikingly the rift that had developed between the regent and the populace that he administered, and his almost blind inability to see the social and political changes that were occurring among the Indonesian people. The regent's remark to Pijper that "the man is well known to me for he is the son of my former *magang*. I am sure Ishak would have reported to me voluntarily had I so requested" demonstrates, as we shall see later, how Kartadiningrat's perception of events in Pandeglang regency was dramatically out of touch with reality.[60]

The rift that had developed between the Resident and the regent did enable the underground PKI in Pandeglang to survive more or less intact up to the November revolt. In Serang and Lebak, where the PKI was anyway largely limited to the town of Rangkasbitung, the rebels suffered crippling blows through the arrests in August and September. There were arrests in Pandeglang, but not on the scale of those in the other two Bantenese regencies. To a great extent the social composition of the underground PKI in Pandeglang assisted the party. As we have seen in Serang regency, the leadership of the PKI tended to consist of artisans and clerks and some skilled workers, although there were of course ulama and jawara as well. In general, the same was true for the PKI in Rangkasbitung. Such people made very easily identifiable targets for the police to follow and eventually to pick up. In Pandeglang regency, on the other hand, leadership of the PKI was almost wholly in the hands

---

59   Interview with Pijper. Kartadiningrat's letter is included as an appendix to his letter of February 7, 1939 to the Governor-General, Vb July 4, 1939 - 19.
60   Ibid.

of ulama and jawara who were far more able to play the role of "fish in water" than the leaders in Serang. The police faced enormous difficulties in unearthing the PKI underground in Pandeglang precisely because of the hold of the ulama and jawara on local villages.

Following the arrests in Serang regency in August and September and that of Afif in Labuan, however, the Veldpolitie were increasingly turning their attention to Pandeglang and making arrests over the heads of the local priyayi, most of whom were too afraid to defy Kartadiningrat. In late September the police arrested Haji Barahim of the village of Bangkujung, Cening, and two other important ulama who had joined the PKI, Kiyai Haji Atje and Kiyai Haji Ilyas of the village of Torogong near Labuan.[61] Other wanted leaders managed to go underground and evade arrest, such as Haji Doelhadi of the village of Bangko who was one of the key leaders of the "DO."[62]

In the meantime Haji Chatib, satisfied that the PKI was at last determined to lead a revolt under the leadership of the Batavia "Komite Pemberontak," worked frantically to prepare the PKI/DO in Pandeglang and also to salvage something of the organization in Serang. This he accomplished, though not without arousing increased police suspicion of his involvement. Partly to deflect police attention, on September 15 Haji Chatib and his brother-in-law, Tb. Haji Emed, reported voluntarily to the police in Serang. They were both released after questioning, having disclaimed any continuing connection with the underground PKI.[63] To some extent Haji Chatib and Tb. Haji Emed enjoyed a greater freedom as a consequence of their relationship to Kiyai Asnawi, at that time one of the most influential religious teachers in West Java, whom Kartadiningrat was exceedingly anxious not to alienate from the government. Indeed, this was a concern shared by even senior Dutch officials. The Governor of West Java, W. P. Hillen, had once written to Putman-Cramer that "great care must be taken that nothing should be done to upset the Kiyai [Asnawi] and his family."[64] By October, however, the Resident felt that there was

61   *De Banten Bode*, October 2, 1926. See also "De Onrust in het Bantamsche," *Java Bode*, October 20, 1926.

62   Haji Doelhadi was eventually arrested in early November in Batavia, *De Banten Bode*, November 6, 1926.

63   "Verklaring Mas Wiria di Koesoema," *De Landsdienaar*, 3, 9 (September 1927), pp. 459-61.

64   Report of Hillen to Governor-General, G13/1/21, January 24, 1927, Mailr 172x/ Vb July 1, 1927 T10.

sufficient evidence to justify arresting Haji Chatib and Tb. Emed. Under questioning in September, Tb. Emed had admitted that he had collected money earlier in the year knowing it was destined for the PKI, and at the monthly serba on October 6 Putman-Cramer asked Kartadiningrat whether he would agree to proceed with the arrest of the two men. The regent resisted, saying that he feared this would provoke widespread social unrest in Banten.[65] Several days later Putman-Cramer complained of the regent' s obstructive attitude in a letter to the West Java Governor Hillen.[66] In advocating extreme caution Kartadiningrat had a formidable ally, however, in the Adviser for Native and Islamic Affairs in Batavia, E. Gobée. At the end of October Gobée wrote a report on the political situation in Banten for the Governor-General's office which strongly criticized the actions of the Resident and of the Veldpolitie. [67] There was a dangerous lack of cooperation between the Dutch and Indonesian administrations in Banten which was not the responsibility of the latter. The knowledge of the priyayi regarding the local situation had to be respected, the adviser argued, if public order was to be maintained in the area.

The Resident, however, had already decided that there was now more than sufficient reason for detaining Haji Chatib, and on October 23 a large contingent of Veldpolitie were sent to Caringin to arrest him. Tb. Emed, who was not taken into custody, hurried to Batavia where he saw Gobée. In a clever ploy aimed at taking advantage of the disagreements within the colonial administration, Tb. Emed admitted to the adviser that he and Haji Chatib had joined the PKI but that this was only because they had felt it was the best organization to promote and protect Islam.[68] Gobée, however, was unable to intervene, and in any case his report was soon to be rudely overtaken by events. The Batavia Komite Pemberontak was now making last-minute preparations for revolt, and on November 6 the final green light was given.[69]

---

65 Statement of R. A. A. Kartadiningrat, April 3, 1927, Mailr 705x/27, Vb July 4, 1939.
66 Report of Hillen, January 24, 1927, see n. 232 above.
67 "Politieke Toestand in het Gewest Bantam," H60, October 29, 1926, Mailr 786x/27.
68 See report of Gobée, "Klachten over het optreden van de politie in het Ban-tamsche," October 31, 1926, H/61, Mailr 786x/27.
69 McVey, Rise, p. 341; Poeze, Tan Malaka, p. 328. The executive of the PKI in Bandung did make one last desperate attempt in November to regain its control over the local sections. At the beginning of the month it sent a circular to all branches calling for purification of the party and a return to centralized leadership by the executive. This initiative was only supported by the Priangan section. See McVey, Rise, p. 342; Poeze, Tan Malaka, p. 328.

MAP 2. LABUAN-MENES AREA

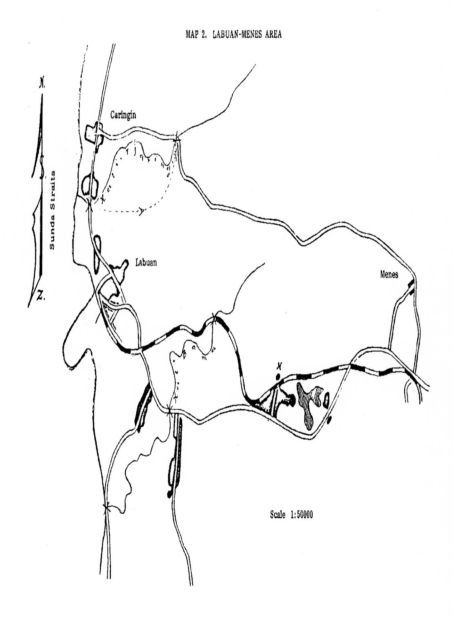

C H A P T E R   T H R E E
THE OUTBREAK OF REVOLT

The last few days before the revolt were marked by frantic activity on both sides. Haji Achmad Chatib's arrest on October 23 had been a bitter blow for the rebels, depriving the PKI of the most important of its leaders still at liberty, while at the same time giving the police fresh leads for their inquiries into the underground PKI in Pandeglang regency. In pursuit of the latter, an officer of the Serang Veldpolitie, Mangoendiwiria, and five policemen were dispatched to Labuan in early November to assist the local police.[1] Several arrests were made and on the morning of November 12 four suspects were sent back to Serang, accompanied by the turncoat former PKI leader, Oesadiningrat, and another policeman, Djaimoen. Only the hapless Djaimoen returned to Labuan that night; Oesadiningrat remained in Serang, thereby escaping almost certain death.[2]

Meanwhile, on the rebel side, Haji Hasan had returned on the evening of November 9 from a meeting with the Batavia PKI leader, Sukrawinata, in the capital. On the way back to Labuan he broke his journey in Serang and Pandeglang to give final instructions to rebel leaders there. The day after his return Haji Hasan visited Tb. Emed in Caringin. Since the arrest of his brother-in-law, Haji Chatib, Tb. Emed had apparently grown increasingly apprehensive about the approaching revolt. On November 9 he had been summoned to Serang once again for questioning, and he

---

1   Interview with Mohammed Djen, one of the policemen referred to in the text, Jakarta, August 20, 1975. Report of Resident of Banten, Putman-Cramer, to Hillen, Governor of West Java, June 27, 1927, no 205G, Mailr 832x/27, Vb September 2, 1927 N14.
2   Report of Hillen to Governor-General de Graeff, January 24, 1927, G13/1/21, Mailr 172x/Vb July 1, 1927 T10.

now feared he would soon follow Chatib into prison. Sensing Tb. Emed's growing unease over the planned insurrection, Haji Hasan dispatched another rebel leader, Haji Saleh, to visit him on the morning of November 11. Haji Saleh's revolutionary credentials were impeccable: his grandfather had been killed in the Haji Wachia revolt of 1850, and his father in the Cilegon revolt of 1888. Haji Saleh outlined the rebel plans to seize first Labuan, Pandeglang, and Serang and then, in order to counter the PKI's numerical weakness in Rangkasbitung, to ferry rebels there by train to take the town. All priyayi and Europeans were to be arrested and those that resisted killed. Once Banten was freed from Dutch rule, the rebels would gather in Caringin, because Kiyai Asnawi was the most influential and important religious leader in the region, and there await further instructions from the PKI insurrectionary committee in Batavia.[3] Despite these last-minute attempts to try and secure Tb. Emed's participation, however, Kiyai Asnawi's son refused to take any further active role in the imminent revolt.

On the morning of November 12 the Labuan market was exceptionally busy as local people stockpiled provisions. For days increased sales of salt and white cloth had been reported throughout Banten, and there were also reports of widespread fasting. That evening several hundred peasants, led by Kiyai Moekri and Kiyai Ilyas, gathered at the village of Bama. Arms which had been stored for months were distributed and duties allocated for the attack on Labuan. The meeting concluded with a "Sembahyang Perang" (war prayer) before the rebels set off for Labuan.[4]

Another large meeting, attended by more than 700 people, had taken place in the village of Pasirlama, near Caringin. The rebels from there, led by Haji Moestapha, were detailed to attack the residence of the Assistant Wedana of Cening.[5] The attack on Menes was to be led by Haji Hasan and Entol Enoh with apparently almost total support from the villages in the area.[6]

Meanwhile, in Serang and Pandeglang rebel bands were also gathering,

---

3   Report of Gobée to Governor-General, December 23, 1927, no. 1/500, Mailr 1484x/27; see also statement of Tb. Emed to police in same report.
4   *De Courant*, January 6, 1927; "Beknopt Overzicht van den actueelen toestand in Bantam," December 9, 1926, G 5/41/15, Mailr 1235x/Vb July 1, 1927 R1O.
5   Interview with Kiyai Abdulhalim; Makmun Salim, "Suatu Tindjauan," pp. 20-21.
6   Interview with Mohammed Djen.

though not with the same degree of cohesion and planning as in Menes and Labuan. In the former towns PKI strength had been fatally weakened in the months preceding the revolt, and Menes and Labuan were to be the center of insurrectionary activity in 1926.

The Attack on Labuan[7]

In Labuan the revolt began just after midnight with an attack by several hundred armed men on the assistant wedana' s residence. The assistant wedana, Mas Wiriadikoesoemah, and his family were taken prisoner by the rebels. A policeman guarding the residence was killed and two others seriously wounded in a gun battle with the rebels.

Following their successful attack the rebels split into two groups. The first supervised the removal of Mas Wiriadikoesoemah to Caringin, while the second searched the streets of Labuan for policemen. This group

---

7   For the course of the 1926 uprising in Banten, besides interviews, I have used the following written sources: Report by Resident of Banten, Putman-Cramer, "Communisten Relletjes in Banten," December 17, 1926, no 412/G, Mailr 45x/27, Vb June 21, 1927 A10; see also the account written by Captain Becking in MvO, J. S. de Kanter, 1934, pp. 67-108; "Verslag over de Relletjes in Menes en Laboean," Report of Regent of Pandeglang, November 14, 1926, appendix 6 to letter of Governor-General to Minister of Colonies, no 395/2 May 22, 1939, Vb July 4, 1939 no 19; "Vervolg van het verslag over de Relletjes in Menes en Laboean," November 29, 1926, Report of Regent of Pandeglang, appendix 9 to preceding document; Mailreports 1101x/26 and 1110x/26 in Vb July 1, 1927 S10 also contain reports by the Governor of West Java, W. P. Hillen, on the 1926 uprising. Of the press coverage of the time I have relied heavily on reports that appeared in De Banten Bode, Bataviaasch Nieuwsblad and De Courant [Bandung]. Where I have used other newspapers I have indicated this in the text. An invaluable series of articles ap-peared in the journal De Landsdienaar throughout 1927 under the heading of "Zaak Mas Wiria di Koesoema." The relevant articles appeared in volume 3, no. 2 (February 1927), p. 129; no. 6 (June 1927), pp. 319-20, 328-29; no. 7/8 (July/August 1927), pp. 375, 377, 387-90; no. 9 (September 1927), pp. 456-63; no. 10 (October 1927), pp. 505-6; no. 11/12 (November/December 1927), pp. 541-42. Other written sources that are useful include "Bantam Report"; Blumberger, Communistische Be-weging, pp. 74-77; Djojopranoto, PKI-SIBAR, pp. 45-49; Pemberontakan Nasional Pertama. A number of articles of interest on the uprising also appeared in the international Communist press of the time. See inter alia "L'insurrection sur Java et ses causes profondes," Le Drapeau Rouge [Bruxelles] , December 18, 19, 20, 1926; Semoan (Semaun), "International Imperialism and the Communist Party of Indonesia, " Communist International, no. 17, 1926; Gerard Vanter [van Munster], "The Insurrection in Java," International Press Correspondence (Inprecorr), vol. 6, no. 80 (November 25, 1926); G. J. van Munster, "The Background and History of the Insurrection in Java," Inprecorr, vol. 6, no. 87 (December 16, 1926); Gerard Vanter, "The Revolts in Indonesia," Inprecorr, vol. 7, no. 5 (January 13, 1927); P. Bergsma, "The Persecution of Revolutionaries in Indonesia," Inprecorr, vol. 7, no. 55 (September 29, 1927); Samim, "The Situation in Indonesia,"Inprecorr, vol. 8, no. 68 (October 4, 1928); Kiyai Samim, "Dutch Imperialist Terror in Indonesia," Inprecorr, vol. 8, no. 57 (August 31, 1928).

went first to the house of Haji Ramal where three policemen from the Serang Veldpolitie were lodging. The men, however, had been alerted by the sound of gunfire in the street and escaped to the beach where they hid until morning. Three other policemen who had just returned from Serang were less fortunate. Arriving just after midnight they ran straight into a large rebel band which left two of them, Djaimoen and Haji Entjeh, dead, and the third, Koesen, severely wounded. The same rebel band attacked the house of Mas Mohammed Dahlan, a clerk who had provided information on the underground PKI to the police, leaving him seriously wounded.

In Menes, the night of revolt claimed even more victims. The main rebel targets were the wedana, Raden Partadinata, the local railway supervisor, Benjamins, and the police. The attack on the wedana's residence began about one o'clock in the morning and involved some 300-400 men. The wedana and a solitary policeman on duty shot several rebels before they were overwhelmed and killed. Another group of rebels had meanwhile seized the railway station and captured Benjamins, the only Dutchman living in the town. Although Benjamins tried to save his life by indicating his willingness to convert to Islam, the mob after some debate decided to take his life, and his severely mutilated body was later found near the railway track.[8] Two policemen were also killed that night, and an attack was made on a retired *patih*. In the village of Cening, midway between Menes and Labuan, another policeman was killed and the assistant wedana shot and wounded.

The Reaction of the Colonial Authorities

Following the attacks on the authorities in Menes and Labuan the initiative in the revolt passed from the hands of the rebels. In the subsequent hours and days, while the rebels remained in control of much of west Banten, their resistance assumed an increasingly reactive character. Although the PKI leadership left at large in Banten in November 1926 had given considerable thought to coordinating their attacks on the police and local government, they had made few plans with regard to what they would do

---

8   Interview with M. Padmadisastra, Rangkasbitung, December 23, 1975.

once these actions were completed.

In some cases even the initial rebel attacks were thwarted by timely action on the part of the authorities. For example in the villages of Cadasari and Baros from where rebel bands were to launch their assault on Pandeglang, the arrival of a large police force at ten in the evening of November 12, prompted local rebel leaders to postpone their action. Even more damaging to the rebels' chance of success was their failure to sever immediately all telephone lines from Labuan and Menes. This resulted in the Regent of Pandeglang being informed of the uprising soon after one in the morning. Ironically, soon after the critical call to Pandeglang had been made, the telephone lines were cut. The authorities in Batavia, however, had already been alerted, and before 4 a.m. a preliminary force of 100 soldiers under Captain Becking had already left for Banten.

In the meantime, Kartadiningrat, the Regent of Pandeglang, together with the local Veldpolitie commander, Martens, and nine policemen, had already left for Menes and Labuan. On the way, the party came under fire from a group of rebels, but they were soon repelled, and the regent's party was able to proceed to Menes. Arriving in the town they found the wedana's residence gutted and Raden Partadinata and three policemen dead. The regent's party now split into two, with Kartadiningrat and Martens and four policemen proceeding to Labuan. There, they made contact with the wedana, who had managed to escape from his residence prior to the rebel attack, and the three police officers, who had spent the night hiding on the beach. Despite some cursory skirmishes with rebel bands throughout the morning no major engagement took place; indeed, Kartadiningrat's small group was even able to carry out some arrests. Around midday the Assistant-Resident of Serang, Westenberg, arrived in Labuan, together with twenty soldiers. The rebels, led by Kiyai Moekri, who had been grouping throughout the morning for an attack on the regent's party now found themselves faced with a more substantial force. Their attack was beaten off and many of them were killed.

Late on the afternoon of November 13 further military reinforcements led by Captain Becking arrived in Labuan. One of the captain's first acts was to dispatch a patrol to Caringin to locate the captured Assistant-Wedana of Labuan, Mas Wiriadikoesoemah, and to arrest Tb. Emed. The patrol, led by Lieutenant van der Vinne, found the assistant-wedana guarded by only one man who offered no resistance. As the patrol approached the house of Tb. Emed, however, they came under heavy gunfire from a nearby warung. In the ensuing battle seven of the rebels inside the hut were shot dead by the soldiers. One rebel appeared to surrender,but, as he approached the patrol, he suddenly attacked them with a long parang, and was shot dead by van der Vinne. The man was later found to be the rebel leader, Haji Saleh. Soon after the engagement the troops left Caringin, returning to Labuan without Tb. Emed, whom they had been unable to find.[9]

The Engagement on November 15

The center of rebel activities from the morning of November 14 was the mosque of the village of Bama, on the outskirts of Labuan. Hundreds of rebels from neighboring villages congregated there from midday on November 14, in expectation of the attack on the Dutch military encampment in Labuan. In speeches to rally their peasant supporters, Kiyai Moekri and other leaders argued that an attack had to be launched on the Dutch in Labuan to avenge the deaths of those who had already fallen in battle.

Throughout that day the rebels made desperate efforts to rally their remaining forces. Kiyai Moekri, who had emerged as the principal rebel leader after the arrest of Haji Chatib, visited Caringin in the morning in an attempt to meet with Tb. Emed. However, this final effort to secure Tb. Emed's adherence to the rebel cause was doomed to failure. Kiyai Asnawi had ordered all his family to remain within his own home and had strictly forbidden Tb. Emed to have any further dealings with the rebels.[10]

The rebel leaders also tried to enlist support for the revolt in villages where it had thus far been lukewarm. Haji Sirad, for example, delivered a letter to a prominent local ulama in the village of Palembang, indicating that Kiyai Asnawi was leading the revolt.[11] Haji Soebari, to whom the

---

9   Police interrogation report of Haji Fadil, son of Kiyai Asnawi, November 20, 1926, Mailr 868x. See also "De Relletjes te Laboean," *De Landsdienaar,* 3, 6 (June 1927), pp. 319-20.

10   Police interrogation report of Haji Fadil.

11   Police interrogation reports of Saingga, November 19, 1926; Kandani, November 22, 1926; Haji Isa, November 19, 1926; and Sapiri, November 22, 1926 (all from the village of Palembang) in Mailr 868x/27.

THE OUTBREAK OF THE REVOLT 83

letter was delivered, refused to go along, retorting that the villagers had no weapons and the Dutch could not simply be blown away. Elsewhere rebel envoys met with more success. Villagers in Pagelaran joined the revolt and killed two local policemen. In the village of Kadugadung a local ulama, Haji Lambri, told his peasant followers that their duty was to support the uprising, for this was not the time to think who was a Communist and who was not, but the rebels should be assisted because they were "our people and Moslems."[12]

Despite the arrival of Dutch reinforcements, the rebels still hoped to overrun Becking's detachments in Labuan, and then to march on to take Pandeglang. During the day of November 14 plans were made for an attack on the Dutch military position in Labuan. In the afternoon the rebels successfully delayed a motorized brigade traveling from Pandeglang as it attempted to enter Labuan. There was a fierce gun battle, but, fortunately for the Dutch, a patrol arrived from Labuan. Attacking the rebels from the rear, it succeeded in dislodging them.

That night the rebels prepared for their second attack on Labuan. They destroyed the bridge over the river Bama and built barricades on either side of the river. Telephone lines out of Labuan were once again cut, and the roads out of the town, east via Menes and north over the Caringin river, were blocked by noon the following day. The rebels also tried to block the railway line.

On the afternoon of the 15th, however, the rebels were caught off guard when their main group of 500 men, making their way to link up with other bands, encountered a patrol led by Becking himself. The rebels were dressed entirely in white with the exception of a black-clothed flag-carrier, a man called Djapar from the village of Bama. Over seventy years of age, Djapar bore a flag with a quotation from the Koran, "With God's help everything can be achieved."[13] The rebels had only a few firearms

---

12 Police interrogation reports of Mirdja, April 14, 1927, and Soedira, December 5, 1926, from the village of Kadugadung, in Mailr 868x/27.

13 See Becking's account, in Kanter, *MvO*, pp. 91-94. A Communist commentator, noting the fact that the rebels were dressed in white, ascribed this to their dedication until death to the cause of the international proletariat; see Vanter, "Insurrection on Java."

On November 15 there were strong rumors of an impending attack on the town of Cilegon. One brigade was sent there, together with a heavy machine-gun unit. See report of Hillen to Governor-General, November 16, 1926, no. G1, Mailr 1110x, Vb July 1, 1927 S10.

and were no match for the Dutch soldiers with their fast-firing carbines. Despite heavy losses the rebels made a futile attempt to surround the military patrol and attack it from two sides, a maneuver which failed due to the Dutch soldiers' tactics of picking off rebel leaders and those with firearms. The rebels were forced to retreat after some twenty-five minutes.[14] They were now completely exhausted and dispirited, having failed in their attack and with many of their leaders dead.

Late the following day, November 16, the Dutch lifted the siege of Labuan when the Governor of West Java, W. P. Hillen, arrived with two more brigades of troops. Further reinforcements came the next day, including an engineering section to repair the bridges. At the same time a gunboat from Batavia with a detachment of marines anchored in Labuan harbor. It spent the subsequent days patrolling the Sunda Straits to prevent the rebels fleeing to Sumatra, an effort which was not entirely successful.

The Revolt in Serang Regency

Although the uprising of November 1926 was largely confined to the Pandeglang regency, the rebels had also planned to attack the town of Serang. Despite the arrests of the Serang PKI leadership in August-September, there was still widespread unrest around the residency capital in November. On the night of November 12 several hundred peasants gathered on the outskirts of the town. The rebels were led by Haji Solichin, Mohammed Tahir, and two well-known jawara, Abdullah and Ayub Achmad. They planned to seize the Resident's office, the police barracks, and the railway station. Although poorly armed, many of the rebels wore "jimat" and had carried out invulnerability rites. They were to await a signal that was to be carried by a messenger on a train from Rangkasbitung. The messenger, however, never arrived, and, after waiting until early morning, the rebels dispersed. Some fifty of them under the leadership of Mohammed Tahir, left for Labuan, but they got only as far as Cimauk before having to hide in the woods to avoid the troops who

---

14   See Becking's account in Kanter, *MvO*, p. 94.

had arrived from Batavia.[15]

The most serious incident in Serang regency occurred at Petir on the night of November 13.[16] The PKI was strong in the area, and had been relatively unaffected by the earlier arrests, unlike the situation in most other regions of Serang regency. As in Pandeglang regency, the local PKI leaders were nearly all religious leaders. Most important among them were Kiyai Emed, Haji Soeeb, Haji Artasik, and Haji Satra. The Petir leaders postponed their action for two days because of the failure of the attack on Serang but they now decided to proceed with their attack on the residence of the Assistant-Wedana of Petir before marching on to Serang. Unknown to them, however, acting on a tip a Dutch military patrol had already taken up positions in Petir and it fought off the attack after a gun battle in which four of the rebels were killed. The rebels' failure at Petir led them to cancel their plans for a general attack on Serang itself and signalled the end of the revolt in the regency.

The Last Days of Resistance

After the street fighting in Labuan on November 15, there was no further serious engagement between the rebels and the Dutch forces, and by November 17 it was clear that the rebel attempt to besiege and overrun the Dutch forces in Labuan had failed. By that date, too, no serious resistance was being offered by the PKI elsewhere in Java. Nevertheless, for several days in Banten some of the rebel groups remained at large, evading arrest and spreading alarming reports in an attempt to maintain some sort of momentum. On the night of November 17 Pandeglang was put on full-scale alert because of widespread rumors of an imminent attack. But the Dutch had now received fresh reinforcements while the rebels had suffered heavy defeats and lost many of their important leaders.

Four brigades of troops left Labuan on November 18 to search the territory south of the town for remaining rebel bands. A fresh brigade

15 Interview with Haji Mohammed Tahir (one of the PKI leaders in Serang in 1926), Serang, December 9, 1975.
16 Police interrogation report of Moekri of the village of Petir, undated, Mailr 868x/Vb April 13, 1928 06. Petir was a former stronghold of the Sarekat Islam in Banten; see *Neratja*, August 1, 1918, and Djajadiningrat, "Politieke Stroomingen."

of Menadonese troops, which had arrived that day, came under fire near the Bama river bridge. They returned the fire and pursued the rebel group into a nearby village. Most of the rebels escaped, but some took refuge in a mosque which the Menadonese troops stormed. Mopping-up operations continued in the area for the next two weeks, but, at the end of the month two armed rebel bands were still apparently in existence, one west of the Pandeglang-Menes road and the second to the east of the road. On the night of December 4 the first of these bands was responsible for setting fire to, and destroying, the house of the headman in the village of Cidolas near Caringin and for beating up a policeman in Cening. Some nights earlier the residences of the assistant-wedana and of the headman of Pagelaran were burned down while their occupants were on patrol outside the village. No further incidents of violence occurred after this. (A mood of sullenness descended on Banten as the population waited apprehensively for Dutch retribution.)

The Revolt outside Banten

The revolt of 1926 was more protracted and assumed a more popular character in Banten than any other region of Indonesia, with the exception of West Sumatra. In other areas of West and Central Java isolated incidents of violence occurred on the night of November 12 and for a few days thereafter, but nowhere did resistance assume the proportions it did in Banten. Even in the Tegal area of Central Java, where local militants had been virulent in their advocacy of armed revolt, arrests by the authorities and the absence of any real plan by the rebels meant that the Communist Party's organization was easily broken and resistance was minimal.[17] In the East Priangan residency of West Java, the PKI mounted a number of attacks on local priyayi and policemen, but on a minor scale compared to the actions in Banten.[18]

Apart from Banten and West Sumatra, the revolt was most serious in

---

17   On Tegal, see "Communistische onlusten te Tegal," Mailr 122x/27, Vb June 21, 1927 A10; Djojoprajitno, *PKI-SIBAR*, pp. 49-56.

18   On the disturbances in the Priangan, see "Beknopt overzicht van de Communistische Ongeregeldheden," Vb December 13, 1926 D19; "Communistische Ongere-geldheden," Vb November 13, 1926 X17.

the capital, Batavia. Indeed, it was only in these three areas that the rebels appears to have acted on the basis of a concerted plan.[19] It is also apparent that many Bantenese played an active role in the revolt in Batavia. Rebel leadership was in the hands of Sukrawinata, Dahlan, Ibu Sukaesih, and Achmad Bassaif. Bassaif had succeeded in recruiting many jawara and jago elements into the PKI from the districts of Jembatan Lima, Tanah Abang, and Kampung Karet, traditional haunts of Bantenese in the capital. The rebels' main targets were in the Kota area of the city, and consisted of Glodok prison and the city telephone exchange, both of which were subjected to a sustained assault. Several policemen were also killed by the rebels in clashes near Tanah Abang railway station and in Mangga Dua. The rebels also captured the telephone exchange for several hours, later escaping by means of the city sewers.[20] However, even in Batavia, resistance was crushed by late on November 14 and a period of arrests and repression ensued.

---

19 For Batavia, see Djajadiningrat, *Herrineringen*, pp. 332-41; interview with Achmad Bassaif, who led the attack on Glodok prison.

20 See the account of the trials of the leaders of this attack in *Bataviaasch Nieuwsblad*, January 19, 20, 21, 22, 24, 25, 27, and 28, 1927.

CHAPTER FOUR
SIGNIFICANT FEATURES OF THE REVOLT IN BANTEN

Certain significant features of the 1926 uprising should be commented upon, although the reasons for the PKI's failure lie largely outside the scope of this study. The revolt in Banten was part of a comprehensive design by the PKI for a concerted attack on the colonial government throughout the Dutch East Indies. Earlier we traced the process by which the Communist Party found itself abandoning all hope of legal political activity in favor of an armed uprising.

It is important to note that the PKI succeeded in Banten in establishing an extensive underground organization that encompassed the regencies of Serang and Pandeglang and the Rangkasbitung area of Lebak regency. This was no mean feat. The degree of revolutionary organization in Banten was more widespread geographically and more encompassing socially than in any other area that participated in the 1926 revolt, with the possible exception of West Sumatra. Compared with the Cilegon revolt of 1888, the degree and extent of organization in 1926 was far greater. In the Cilegon uprising, by far the most serious revolt in Banten during the nineteenth century, the rebel organization was confined to the western half of Serang regency, and the rest of the region was completely unaffected.[1] By contrast, the revolutionary organization in 1926 enveloped almost the whole of the residency of Banten with the exception of the regency of Lebak. Lebak was the most sparsely populated regency in Java and, outside the environs of the town of Rangkasbitung, where the PKI was well entrenched, the peasantry were engaged almost wholly in slash and

---

1 See Sartono, *Peasants' Revolt*, p. 233.

burn (*huma*) rice production. The rubber plantations in the regency were worked by a labor force that was almost entirely drawn from Central Java. Even in Lebak, however, the insurrectionaries intended to make good their lack of strength by transporting rebels by train from Labuan to Rangkasbitung after Labuan had been captured.

The area of the actual revolt was, as we have seen, largely limited to the regency of Pandeglang, in particular to the Menes-Labuan area, and to the Petir district of Serang regency. But it is clear that a serious insurrection would have occurred in Serang regency had it not been for the crippling wave of arrests that took place in August and September. If we examine the list of Bantenese exiled to Boven Digul (see Appendix I) we can see that most of those recommended for internment without trial were arrested before the revolt, and the majority came from Serang regency. The Dutch authorities themselves were very clear about this. The Governor of West Java, W. P. Hillen, wrote to the Governor-General, A. C. D. de Graeff, in April 1927:

> If one thinks [of the situation] in North Banten, the inclination and propensity to revolt was much greater than in Pandeglang, and if it were not for the timely and strong reaction of the administration the results would have been much worse than now in Pandeglang.[2]

It is evident, then, that social and political unrest in 1926 was far more widespread than the acts of rebellion in which it eventually manifested itself. As the Committee of Inquiry into the revolt noted, the important fact about the unrest of 1926 was not so much that there was a revolt in Labuan, Menes, and Petir, but that in a far greater number of places a large number of people were prepared to revolt.[3] Indeed, it is striking that there were fewer members of the PKI in the rebellious areas of Labuan, Menes, and Petir than in the region of Serang-Taktakan-Gunungsari which did not join the uprising. Anyer and Cilegon were also important centers of PKI activity which did not participate in the final uprising.

---

2   Hillen to Governor-General, April 8, 1927, G13/4/8, Mailr 705x, Vb July 4, 1939.
3   "Bantam Report," p. 40.

The loss at a late stage of the single most important rebel leader, Haji Achmad Chatib, also probably limited the extent of rebel violence. Chatib's arrest, together with the last-minute faint-heartedness of Tb. Emed, seriously weakened the PKI leadership in Banten. Chatib's participation alone, despite the earlier arrests in Serang, might have still galvanized the rebel ranks in that regency into joining with the Pandeglang rebels. As a commentator noted after the revolt:

> No one can have any doubt that the rebellion would have had a much more serious character had it not been for the arrests that took place before November 12. This is particularly so when one looks at Achmad Chatib. If, as the rebels planned, he had led the revolt it would have been much more extensive and would probably have spread throughout Banten.[4]

With Chatib' s participation, the rebels might well have succeeded in their plans for the seizure of Labuan and Menes followed by a joint march on Pandeglang, where they would have been assisted in their attack on the town by bands, led by Kiyai Madun of Petir, advancing from the north and northeast, and by others, led by Kiyai Achmad of Pancur (Serang).

It is virtually impossible to ascertain the total number of adherents to the rebel cause. The police estimated that there were approximately four thousand PKI members in Banten, but this figure was far smaller than the number of people who had bought membership cards and who considered themselves to be part of the revolutionary organization.[5] As early as February 1926, as noted earlier, Dutch intelligence reports estimated PKI support in Banten at more than twelve thousand. Indeed, Captain Becking, the military commander during the revolt, estimated that as many as fifteen thousand rebels were active in the Menes-Labuan region alone. It is true that the number of rebels involved in the attacks on the residences of civil servants was in fact never more than several hundred, a feature that also characterized the uprising of 1888, but this had as much to do with poor mobilization of the rebel supporters

---

4   *De Courant*, January 5, 1927.
5   "Bantam Report," p. 40.

as anything else. From other sources it is clear that the total number of peasants who considered themselves to be members of the PKI exceeded fifty thousand throughout Banten.[6]

An examination of the social composition of the rebel forces reveals a number of interesting points. First, the group of artisans and clerks who had so much to do with bringing the PKI to Banten, and who provided the first cadres for the party in the region, did not participate in the November insurrection. This group, small in number, and probably the only group with any serious understanding of the aims and ideology of the PKI, had almost all been arrested in August and September 1926. The few individuals who escaped arrest, such as Achmad Bassaif, had left Banten for Batavia. Although this group of secular Communists had been instrumental in establishing the PKI, and also the illegal "DO" organization, in Banten the leadership of both passed to the traditional practitioners of rebellion in the region, namely the ulama or religious leaders. In that sense the leaders of the final revolt in November 1926 were not markedly different from the leaders of earlier rebellions in Banten in the nineteenth century. What was different was that the religious leaders were coopted into a revolutionary organization that was not of their making or design and which for the first time not only encompassed the whole of Banten but also had wide-reaching connections throughout Java and Sumatra.

It is clear that, in addition to the ulama, the jawara played an important role in the revolt. Indeed, the large number of policemen who died in the November uprising may well have been due, in part, to a settling of old scores by some of the jawara. Their participation in the revolt, given their scant regard for the authorities and the laws of the land, is perhaps not surprising. What is noteworthy, however, is that the PKI had been able to coopt them into the revolutionary organization, when in other contexts and in other countries such elements have proven far too individualistic to be drawn into political or social movements. There was in Banten, as we have pointed out before, a long tradition of brigandage and social banditry, which, although it contributed to the unruliness of the region, did not lend itself easily to participation in acts of rebellion. Although, for

---

6   Interviews with former members of the PKI as well as with local priyayi.

example, the 1880s was a decade in which banditry appears to have been quite widespread in Banten, there is almost no evidence that these bandits were drawn to the 1888 Cilegon uprising. The majority of participants in the 1926 revolt were, of course, ordinary peasants. Visitors to Banten after the revolt were struck by the fact that whole villages in the Menes and Labuan areas had simply been deserted by their peasant dwellers.

The most obvious targets of the rebels were the priyayi. In particular, it was police officials who were killed unsparingly by the rebels. Against civil servants as a whole the rebels were more selective. The Wedana of Menes, Raden Partadinata, who was not Bantenese and who had a reputation for being repressive, was killed by the rebels as the Assistant-Wedana of Menes would almost surely have been if he had been apprehended. In Labuan, however, the assistant-wedana merely kidnapped and held captive. A number of factors were probably involved in the sparing of Mas Wiriadikoesoemah's life. He was a local man and seemingly widely respected. Moreover, as we noted earlier, in September he had warned one of the local PKI leaders, Afif, of his impending arrest. Popular resentment against the civil service also found expression in the course of the revolt in the destruction of government archives and the houses of officials.

The only Dutchman to be killed in the course of the revolt was Benjamins, the railway supervisor in Menes. Benjamins was one of the few Europeans living in the Menes-Labuan area and was unpopular locally for an allegedly hostile attitude towards the PKI and also towards the Sarekat Islam earlier. Additionally he upset local values by living openly with a Bantenese woman to whom he was not married. Against local Chinese there was no visible hostility in the course of the insurrection, as had also been true in the Cilegon uprising of 1888. Although there had been some attacks on Chinese in August and September, this was not repeated in the actual rebellion of November 1926. In this respect social unrest in the Banten region was markedly different from that in neighboring Tangerang.[7] On the morning of November 13, when the rebels were gathering their forces for an assault on the Dutch military position in Labuan, the Chinese population left the town en masse, indicating that they may well have been forewarned by the rebels. There is also

---

7   See Rapport over de Tangerangsche Ratoe Adil Beweging, 1924, passim (in my possession).

considerable evidence that Chinese traders in Banten, and particularly in Menes and in Labuan, had sold arms and ammunition to the rebels, in some cases knowing the purpose to which it would be put. There were also at least two local Chinese who were prominent members of the PKI. One of them, Tju Tong Hin, had belonged to the PKI in Rangkasbitung and was later exiled to Boven Digul.

The absence of any attacks on the Chinese who monopolized much of local trade, especially in the coconut-growing area of Labuan, would seem to indicate the absence of class conflict as a specific theme of the revolt. Many of the rebels themselves reportedly belonged to the ranks of rich peasants and others were traders. This did not prevent them from participating in the rebellion or from considering their objectives to be the same as those of the other participants in the revolt. But it should be noted that in August and September there had been pressure, and in some cases attacks, on Chinese and wealthy haji and, in Petir at least, one murder of a well-to-do trader by the underground PKI.

Before examining the outcome of the revolt we should note the achievements of the rebels, temporary and short-lived though they were. In the first place, at least briefly, the insurrectionaries effectively held the Menes-Labuan area. In Labuan they successfully isolated the troops sent to suppress the revolt for a few days and almost succeeded in overrunning their positions. The rebel forces, however, were almost entirely composed of ordinary peasants who were not prepared to see a long campaign through. Moreover, the peasants' leaders had no far-reaching plans of what to do next. The most they hoped for were instructions from the executive revolutionary leadership in Batavia. Only as long as no effective armed force stood against them could they maintain their position. In actual armed clashes the rebels inevitably conceded defeat, often after a desultory exchange. To some extent they were undoubtedly blinded by their conviction that they were invulnerable in waging the jihad against the infidel Dutch, being fortified in this conviction by the belief that they were part of a nationwide insurrection against colonial rule. For the first time Banten had risen in revolt, not in isolation but as part of a national movement against colonial oppression.

CHAPTER FIVE

SEQUEL TO THE REVOLT

Tension remained high throughout the region in the weeks after the revolt because of the wave of arrests,and it was fueled further by rumors of a new revolt. New insurrections were supposed to break out on the night of December 6. Other rumors suggested that the wedana and assistant-wedana would not have sufficient money to pay the soldiers, who would therefore withdraw to Batavia, leaving the priyayi once again exposed to new murderous assaults.[1] Despite the arrests and the rumors, by the end of the first week of December most of the villages in the Menes-Labuan area were repopulated, though still with a significant absence of men, many having apparently fled to Batavia or across the Sunda Straits to the Lampungs, either because of their participation in the revolt or from fear of arrest.

Up to November 13 the authorities in Banten had made sixty-seven arrests in connection with the underground PKI, fifty-six in Serang regency, five in Lebak, and five in Pandeglang. Between November 13 and December 8, there were a further 916 arrests, 134 in Serang regency, one in Lebak, and 781 in Pandeglang. These figures, however, do not include many hundreds more detained for interrogation and released after several days or, in some cases, weeks.[2] As the total arrests throughout Indonesia in connection with the 1926 revolt was 13,000, the Banten figure of approximately 1,300 accounted for 10 percent of these. Even given that

---

1   See the report of the Governor of West Java, W. P. Hillen, "Beknopt verslag van den actueelen toestand in Bantam," December 9, 1926, G. 5/41/15, Mailr 1235x/ 26, Vb July 1, 1927 R10; *Bataviaasch Nieuwsblad*, December 4, 1926. These rumors persisted into 1927. In May of that year, police received reports of a new underground PKI emerging in Banten. See "Maandlijksche Politieke Overzicht April-May 1927," Mailr 677x and 930x, Vb August 24, 1928 H14.

2   Hillen, "Beknopt verslag."

Banten was one of the main centers of the revolt, this was a very high percentage when it is remembered that the population of the district at the time was 900,000 out of a total Indonesian population of some 60 million. Indeed, as the total number of arrests in all of West Java was just 3,000, Banten's proportion was extremely high. By contrast, the number of arrests in West Sumatra, a much wider area, was 2,000.

Nevertheless, many of the rebels were in fact lucky. Many who had simply been ordinary party members or who had participated in the revolt managed to escape arrest, provided they were not betrayed by spies or by comrades under interrogation.[3] Of the important figures in the insurrectionary movement, there are three whose escape we should note. One was Kiyai Moekri who, after the arrest of Haji Chatib, assumed leadership of the revolutionary movement in the Labuan area. Kiyai Moekri fled first to Ciruas, east of Serang, where he was sheltered by another ulama who had taken no direct part in the revolt, Kiyai Rafiuddin. From there he made his way to Surabaya in East Java and eventually, disguised as a pilgrim, fled to Mecca where he adopted the name Sech Kabir. He returned to Banten only in the 1960s at the invitation of President Sukarno.[4]

Another group of Bantenese rebels, about ten in number, fled via Palembang to Malaya, where they lived for many years.[5] The most prominent among them were Tje Mamat, chairman of the Anyer PKI subsection, and Tb. Alipan. In Malaya Tje Mamat and Alipan were to fall under the influence of the newly established PARI, a breakaway Communist political group founded by Tan Malaka, Subakat, and Djamaluddin Tamin.

Apart from Kiyai Moekri and the small group who escaped to Malaya, most of the other rebel leaders faced retribution from the colonial authorities. Many were brought before the courts to receive long prison

---

3   Interview with Haji Solichin, Serang, March 14, 1976.
4   Interview with Kiyai Turmudi, son of Kiyai Rafiuddin, Serang, May 11, 1976. Kiyai Moekri was reported to be in Jeddah in October 1927, together with another Bantenese rebel Haji Tajib, by the Dutch consul, van der Meulen. The Netherlands Indies authorities contemplated seeking their extradition but Gobée advised against this. See his report, No I/457a, November 21, 1927, Mailr 1377x/27. Kiyai Moekri returned to Banten in 1964 and died in Menes in February 1967.
5   Interviews with Tje Mamat and Tb. Alipan. See also Tamin, *Sedjarah PKI*, pp. 43, 52.

sentences and in four cases the death penalty.[6] Some 700 men were sentenced to imprisonment, ranging from two years to life.[7] Another group, ninety-nine in number, against whom there was not sufficient evidence to prefer charges in open court, were interned indefinitely in the notorious camp at Boven Digul in New Guinea (see Appendix I). Some would never leave there alive and others had to wait for nearly twenty years, until 1945, before they were able to return to their homes and families in Banten. Among those interned in Boven Digul were all the important PKI leaders in Banten, including Haji Achmad Chatib, Puradisastra, Achmad Bassaif, Tb. Hilman, and Agus Soleiman.[8]

What is perhaps most striking in examining the list of ninety-nine Bantenese who were exiled to Boven Digul (see Appendix I) is the close identity between communism in Banten and religion; Eleven out of the ninety-nine interned were religious teachers, while twenty-seven out of the ninety-nine, nearly one-third, were haji. This was a very high proportion, particularly when we bear in mind that out of the first thousand persons exiled to Boven Digul from all over Indonesia only fifty-nine were haji.[9] Even more relevant is that, of the twenty-seven exiled haji, seventeen had spent at least a year in the Holy Land and some two or three years. This group included Haji Achmad Chatib, who had spent three years in Mecca, Haji Abdulhamid (Adung), Haji Asgari, Haji Artadjaja, Haji Emed, Haji Soeeb, Haji Abdulhadi, Haji Akjar, Haji Mohammed Arif, Haji Mu'min, Haji Aliasgar, Haji Mardjuk, Haji Santani, Haji Achmad, and Haji Enggus. Haji Mohammed Arif had spent a total of five years in Mecca. Achmad Chatib' s younger brother Haji Abdulhamid (Adung), in

---

6   The four men executed were Haji Asikin, Doelsalam, Jamin, and Jas'a. Haji Asikin was found guilty of the murder of two orderlies of the Assistant-Wedana of Menes; Doelsalam and Jamin received the death penalty for their part in the killing of Benjamins, and Jas'a was found guilty of the murder of the Wedana of Menes. The executions were carried out in Pandeglang prison on September 16, 1927. See De Banten Bode, September 17, 1927.

7   See report of Gobée to the Director of Justice, February 8, 1928, No 5/49 G, Mailr 868x/1928; Blumberger, Communistische Beweging, p. 111. In May 1927 some 300 detainees in Banten were released for lack of evidence against them; see De Banten Bode, May 21, 1927.

8   Puradisastra first served a prison sentence of five years and ten months and Bassaif an eight-year sentence before being exiled to Boven Digul. For Puradisastra's trial see De Courant, January 14, and De Banten Bode, January 15, May 21, 1927. For Bassaif' s trial for leading the attack on Glodok prison in Batavia, see Bataviaasch Nieuwsblad, January 19, 20, 21, 22, 24, 25, 27, and 28, 1927.

9   W. M. F. Mansvelt, "Onderwijs en Communisme," Koloniale Studien, 12, 2 (April 1928), p. 218.

addition to two years in Mecca, had spent a further year at the Al-Azhar school in Cairo. While this was already not so unusual in many parts of Sumatra, Haji Abdulhamid was one of the very first Bantenese to go to the famous Islamic educational center in Egypt.

Nearly all the ninety-nine internees were local people, only eight coming from outside the region of Banten. Of them, three were important PKI leaders, Puradisastra (No. 14), Hasanuddin (No. 51), and Atmodihardjo (No. 87) who was from Yogyakarta in Central Java. The other five outsiders were Mohammed Ali (No. 21), who had been born in Banjarmasin (Kalimantan); Tju Tong Hin (No. 37), the only Chinese to be interned from Banten who, despite his ethnic background, had been an important PKI leader in Rangkasbitung; Tjondrosaputro (No. 70), a trader from Central Java who had been chairman of the PKI subsection in Rangkasbitung; Salihun (No. 73), a shoemaker from Batavia, who had been an important PKI propagandist in Banten; and Mohammed Saleh (No. 86), a policeman from Purworejo in Central Java, whose arrest in August had sparked off a purge of the Serang PKI leaders. Seventy-nine of those arrested were resident at the time in Serang regency (thirteen in Pandeglang regency, and five in Lebak regency), and another two had already fled from Serang to Batavia. The disproportionately high percentage of internees from Serang regency reflects two things: first, because the revolt was centered in Pandeglang regency, many of the PKI leaders there were tried in open court rather than being sent for indefinite detention to Boven Digul; second, it also reflects the sweeping wave of arrests carried out by the police in August and September 1926.

What is very clear, however, is the breadth of the PKI organization in the Banten region. Nearly every district in the residency is represented in the list of exiles. The only districts conspicuously absent are the sparsely populated southern regions of Lebak and Pandeglang. It is evident from the list, then, that the PKI underground was well established throughout Banten and was not limited to those districts where an actual armed revolt occurred on the night of November 12, 1926. Indeed, it is of interest to note that more than half of the ninety-nine men interned in Boven Digul had been arrested by the authorities before November 12.[10]

---

10   For the dates of the arrests see Appendix I.

With what sort of picture of the social composition of the Communist movement in Banten does the list of internees present us? The close ties between the PKI in Banten and local religious leaders have already been noted. It is not surprising, then, that nine of those interned were prominent local ulama. Also present on the list are a significant number of artisans, some of whom had joined the PKI outside Banten. This group is represented by five clerks, two printers, three tailors, a shoemaker, a bricklayer, a barber, and an auctioneer. The most numerous occupational groupings, however, are peasants (fifty-four) and traders (thirteen).

These occupational categories, however, are often rather deceptive. This is often the case with the traders. If we look more closely at the police interview records we come across lives that were precarious, involving shifts from one area to another and from one job to another. Frequently an individual moved from one occupation to another or even tried to carry out two or more at the same time. Haji Enggus (No. 9), for example, was a small-time trader in copra, yet at the same time he also ran a retail shop and gave religious education to youngsters in his village. Surabaita (no. 64), although only a young man of twenty, had already worked as a clerk in Ceribon, and had then moved to Buitenzorg (Bogor) where he found work as an apprentice mechanic; he had finally opened a small tobacco-store in Pandeglang. Dulah (No. 60), aged 35, had spent the larger part of his working life as a peasant, but he had apparently been forced to sell his lands and had then worked successively as a sharecropper, a hawker, and a bricklayer. As with many of the others, however, Dulah often moved back and forth between these occupations. This occupational precariousness seems to have been as marked among the educated PKI leaders as among their peasant following. Arman (No. 15) had attended a local school in Serang and then taught as a village schoolteacher in Pontang, worked as a clerk in Telukbetung, and then as a tobacconist in Serang.

Thirteen of the internees listed their profession as trader. This term, "handelaar" in the Dutch police record, tells us little, however, of the person's wealth, the success of his enterprise, and the degree to which he was engaged in commercial activity. For some of the group we have somewhat more detailed information. Ibing (No. 24), for example, who was a PKI propagandist in Menes, had earned his living first as a sailor, then as a fisherman, and finally as a tailor. His final occupation made him a "tradesman" in the Dutch records yet, as with many of the others, it should not be taken as indicating that the PKI in Banten reflected the emergence of a commercialized section of the peasantry, as has been argued for West Sumatra.[11] On the contrary, the "traders" often seem to have been landless peasants who had moved to Batavia or Sumatra and entered a trade there, which they later tried to pursue in Banten. Mohammed Nur Fas Nani (No. 36), who owned no land, had left Banten as a young man to work as a laborer in Batavia. Finding times hard in the early 1920s, he returned home to work with his father who owned a small tobacco stall in Serang. The stall, however, did not make sufficient money to maintain both Nani and his father, so went back to Batavia to seek work as a coolie. After a few months he returned again to Banten, and this time he found employment as a servant in Serang. Even the one Chinese from Banten to be interned, Tju Tong Hin, seems to have become a trader only when he could find no other employment. Tju Tong Hin had previously worked as a laborer in the railway workshops in Meester Cornells, then as a small trader in Tangerang before returning to Batavia to find work as a tinsmith. After a few years in the capital he moved to Banten, earning his living as a fisherman. But it seems that this occupation also brought him little more success than his previous jobs and, taking advantage of a loan from a relative in Rangkasbitung, he opened a small stall in the market town.

The impression one gets of the Bantenese traders who joined the PKI is that many of them had engaged in trade at a time when economic expectations were rising as a result of the post-World War I boom. When economic conditions began to deteriorate, as they did markedly after 1920, many of the newcomers to trading activities found themselves exposed to the cold wind of depression. Haji Achmad Chatib, for example, had earned his living by trading in cloth and timber between 1919 and 1922. It seems, however, that he always had great difficulty in making ends meet, and in 1922 he went bankrupt. Two years later he tried to resume his trading activities, this time dealing in hides, but apparently with no more success. A similar picture emerges from the story of the life of Abdul Kahal bin Haji Osman, a Bantenese Communist arrested

---

11   See the Introduction by Harry Benda and Ruth T. McVey, to their *Communist Revolts of 1926-27*, pp. xi-xxxi; B. Schrieke, "The Causes and Effects of Communism on the West Coast of Sumatra," *Indonesian Sociological Studies,* Pt. 1 (Bandung: van Hoeve, 1960), pp. 83-167.

in West Sumatra. At the age of fourteen he had followed his brother to Muara Amin in West Sumatra. At the age of sixteen he became a small trader in the Lampungs but after nine months he gave up, returning first to Banten and then, unable to find work, to Menggani on Sumatra's west coast. He stayed here for one year working as a share-cropper and then moved back to Banten, where he lived with relatives for a further two years. In 1923 he returned to West Sumatra and began trading in *kain*. Because this did not provide him with a reasonable living, he eventually again gave up trade and became a peasant near Muara Amin.[12]

Peasants, however, formed the largest single occupational group among the internees. This was a cause of concern to senior Dutch officials, and Hillen, Governor of West Java, wrote in September 1927 of his misgivings to the Governor-General:

> What is most striking is that the majority of the rebels belong to the mass of the population. There are few intellectuals or semi-intellectuals. More than half of the rebels have received no education … most noticeable is the very large number of peasants.[13]

Hillen noted that only twenty-two of the internees from Banten had received any form of secular education. Of this number only seven had attended the elementary school in Dutch (HIS).[14] Hillen feared that the large number of Bantenese peasants would be too easily influenced by the "Batavia and Bandung intellectuals" in Boven Digul. As the ninety-nine detainees had already spent almost a year in prison, the Governor felt that some of their number might be sentenced to some form of conditional or suspended internment. This idea, however, was firmly opposed by the Resident of Banten, Putman-Cramer.[15] The Resident argued that the internees must be measured not by their education but by their degree of influence in their native villages. Although Hillen still had strong misgivings, which were supported by Gobée, they were overruled by the

---

12 Mailr 1051x/27.
13 Hillen to Governor-General, September 24, 1927, G 5/74/14, Mailr 637x/28.
14 These included Tb. Hilman, Afif, Achmad Rifai, Ishak, and Surabaita.
15 Putman-Cramer to Hillen, October 21, 1927, No 500/G, Mailr 637x/28; Hillen to Governor-General, November 1, 1927, G 5/85/14, Mailr 637x/28.

objections of Putman-Cramer who was energetically supported by the powerful Director of Justice, Rutgers.[16]

The fifty-four peasants who were eventually interned were nearly all illiterate. It seems from the police records of their interviews that most had worked on their fathers' fields, sometimes until they were quite old. This accounted for the fact that at least eight of them had never been outside their village. Others, whose parents were perhaps too poor to support an extra hand on the fields, had moved to Batavia as young men to seek laboring work. They returned when they had amassed a little money and then sought some land to buy or engaged in sharecropping.

The peasants were all asked during their interrogation why in fact they had joined the Communist Party. Although one must treat their answers with a certain degree of reservation, it is striking how many refer to the burden of taxation and/or to the examples set by others in their village. Thus Bakri (No. 95) joined "because most of my neighbors had done so."[17] Haji Mohammed Jaisin of Anyer joined the PKI because "many of my fellow villagers had bought cards and I didn't want to be left out." Another joined the party as he otherwise "feared that some calamity would overcome me," while another plaintively confessed that he had become a member of the PKI "because life was so difficult and I hoped in this way to get myself out of difficulties."[18]

In the other residencies few peasants were interned. Indeed, one of the main conclusions that Mansvelt drew in his study of the social origins of the detainees was that they had enjoyed a better education than was normal and came from comparatively affluent backgrounds.[19] "The Communist leaders," he wrote, "belong not only to the thin upper layer [of Indonesian society] who have received some education, but more

---

16 In October the Procureur- Generaal advised against any conditional or suspended internment order but felt there was a strong case for some of the Bantenese to be released on the grounds that they were not an immediate danger to the public order. See Procureur-Generaal to Governor of West Java, October 7, 1927, No 2349 AP. This proposal was supported by Gobée in a letter of February 8, 1928 to the Director of Justice Rutgers, No 5/49 G, Mailr 637x/28.

17 Mailr 1105x/27.

18 Ibid.

19 Mansvelt, "Onderwijs en Communisme," pp. 203-25. Mansvelt's study was based on 1,000 of the detainees of whom eighty-eight were Bantenese. By the end of 1927 some 1,300 political prisoners had been interned in Boven Digul because of their alleged involvement in the 1926-27 uprisings, ninety-nine of them Bantenese.

specifically to the even smaller group who have attended the second-class school and enjoyed Western lower education. If there is a certain connection between a definite education and political militancy, then it is the native second-class school which was attended by 447 of the Communists [of the one thousand examined]."[20] In Banten, as we have seen, only a tiny minority of the Communist movement fitted the picture described by Mansvelt.

The detainees from Banten, then, were on the whole less well-educated and from lower-class backgrounds than those from other areas of Indonesia. Indeed, the majority of internees from Banten were ordinary peasants. This finding is consistent with the fact that the revolt of November 1926 had a more popular base in Banten than any other region, with the exception of West Sumatra. In other areas of Java and Sumatra, the PKI mass base had been progressively whittled away throughout 1925 and 1926, leaving it a thoroughly emaciated body. The events of November 1926-January 1927 showed convincingly that the party no longer possessed any degree of mass support except in those two areas most tested by revolt, Banten and West Sumatra.

---

20 Ibid., pp. 211-12. See also reports in Mailr 359x/27.

APPENDIX ONE
LIST OF PERSONS FROM BANTEN
EXILED TO BOVEN DIGUL

	Name	Age	Occupation	Place of Birth	Residence	Particulars
1.	Tb. K. H. Achmad Chatib	31	Religious teacher	Gajam, Pandeglang	Caringin	Chairman of Sarekat Islam-Labuan; Assistant Chairman of the PKI-Section Banten; Religious President of the PKI Banten (President Agama). Son-in-law of Kiyai Asnawi. Studied three years in Mecca. (Arrested October 22, 1926.)
2.	Tb. H. Abdulhamid (Adung)	23	Religious teacher	Idem	Cikondang, Pandeglang	Brother of H. Achmad Chatib. Both sons of K. H. Waseh. Spent one year at Al-Azhar (Cairo). Urged his followers to fast for five days and annointed them with holy water to make them invulnerable.
3.	K. H. Mohammed Gozali	38	Religious teacher	Sanding, Pamarayan	Sanding, Pamarayan	Influential local leader of PKI; collected 200 guilders for the purchase of weapons; told his followers the purpose of the revolt was the murder of Europeans because of the burden of taxes on the people. Brother of Kiyai H. Emed of Petir.
6.	H. Abdullah	40	Peasant	Koranji, Serang	Koranji, Serang	Arrested October 12, 1926.

Name	Age	Occupation	Place of Birth	Residence	Particulars
7. H. Mohammed Arif	30	Village head	Karundang, Serang	Dalung, Serang	Dismissed as village head because he Arif head Serang Serang was a Communist agitator. Active member of the "Dubbel Organisatie" (DO) . His brother H. Mohammed Ali was killed in the fighting of Petir. Arrested November 26, 1926.
8. H. Mohammed Jaisin	35	Peasant	Labuan, Anyer	Labuan, Anyer	PKI courier; influential propagandist, visited houses after evening prayers. Arrested March 10, 1927.
9. H. Enggus	48	Trader	Baru, Cilegon	Warnasari, Cilegon	Arrested February 1, 1927.
10. H. Santani	25	Tailor	Jombangwetan, Cilegon	Kebonsari, Cilegon	Arrested February 11, 1927.
11. H. Soeeb	35	Peasant	Petir, Pamarayan	Petir, Pamarayan	One of the leaders of the attack on Petir. Also collected support for an attack on Serang.
12. H. Artadjaja	25	Peasant	Pancaregang, Cilegon	Pancaregang, Cilegon	Declared in his village that all civil servants from village head to Resident should be killed. Arrested November 4, 1926.
13. H. Ayip Achmad	26	Small trader	Lontar, Serang	Lontar, Serang	Leading member of PKI-DO.
14. Puradisastra	35	C l e r k , journalist	C i s o m p e t , Negara (East Priangan)	Serang	"Father of Bantenese Communism." Chairman of PKI-Section Banten. Established Printers' Union and Drivers' Union in Batavia in 1924. Self-educated.
15. Arman	30	Clerk trader	Karegnen, Serang	Sopeng, Serang	Brother of Alirachman (see below). Collected 470 guilders for the purchase of firearms.

Name	Age	Occupation	Place of Birth	Residence	Particulars
16. Alirachman	28	Auctioneer	Idem	Serang	Secretary PKI-Section Banten; Commissar PKI-DO. Arrested August 16, 1926.
17. Tb. Hilman	27	Clerk—Landrent Office	Mengger, Pandeglang	Kaujon, Serang	Educated Serang HIS. Established Rukun Asli; Commissaris PKI-Section Banten. Arrested September 24, 1926.
18. [Agus] Soleiman	36	Clerk	Rancapare, Serang	Idem	Commissaris PKI-Section Banten. , Arrested August 15, 1926.
19. H. Radi	40	Peasant	Kepuh, Anyer	Kasambironjok, Anyer	Close associate of Tje Mamat, secretary of PKI chapter in Anyer. Urged peasants to revolt because of the tax burden. Arrested December 13, 1926.
20. Dulhamid	45	Peasant	Pabuaran, Ciomas	Pabuaran, Ciomas	Arrested November 6, 1926.
21. Mohammed Ali	38	Peasant	Banjarmasin (Kalimantan)	Bandulu, Anyer	Arrested December 13, 1926.
22. Sentot	24	Peasant	Sudimampir, Anyer	Sudimampir, Anyer	Sudimampir, Former sailor; PKI propagandist. Adjutant to Tje Mamat, PKI leader who fled abroad after revolt. Arrested October 13, 1926.
23. Wajut	32	Peasant and trader	Idem	Idem	Well-known gambler and jawara. PKI propagandist. Arrested October 12, 1926.

	Name	Age	Occupation	Place of Birth	Residence	Particulars
24.	Ibing	30	Tailor	Murui, Menes	Murui, Menes	PKI propagandist, using as a cover his tailor's shop and *main gambus* (Arabic dancing) . Arrested October 12, 1926.
25.	Kasan	40	Peasant, ex-village head	Kosambironjok, Anyer	Gunungsih, Anyer	PKI propagandist. Arrested October 12, 1926.
26.	Moechamad Noer	30	Clerk	Sudimampir, Anyer	Sudimampir, Anyer	Clerk at the PKI office in Serang. Arrested October 12, 1926.
27.	Daud	50	Peasant and trader	Petir, Pamarayan	Petir, Pamarayan	PKI propagandist. Took part in the attack on Petir. Former leader of Sarekat Islam in Banten. Arrested December 20, 1926.
28.	Abdulmalik	56	Trader	Idem	Idem	Former leader of Sarekat Islam in Banten. Owner of a stall that was used for propaganda purposes. Arrested December 20, 1926.
29.	Ibrahim	40	Peasant	Pancaregang, Ciomas	Pancaregang, Ciomas	PKI propagandist, encouraged people to fast in preparation for the revolt. Arrested November 2, 1926.
30.	Dulmuin	45	Peasant	Idem	Kadugenep, Pamarayan	Influential PKI activist among the peasants. Former Sarekat Islam activist. Fasted one month before revolt. Participated in Petir attack. Gathered men for attack on Wedana of Pamarayan's residence. Arrested March 8, 1927.
31.	Durakim	40	Peasant	Gunungsari, Ciomas	Gunungsari, Ciomas	PKI promoter. Arrested October 7, 1926.
32.	Soleman	28	Peasant	Ciomas	Idem	PKI promoter. Well-known jawara. Recruited by Tb. Hilman and charged with ensuring security of secret PKI meetings. Arrested October 22, 1926.
33.	Umar	39	Peasant, ex-village head	Kaduagung, Ciomas	Kaduagung, Ciomas	Arrested October 23, 1926.

	Name	Age	Occupation	Place of Birth	Residence	Particulars
34.	Kasiman	23	Peasant	Sindangmandi, Ciomas	Sindangmandi, Ciomas	Arrested November 6, 1926.
35.	Martadjani	25	Peasant	Pabuaran, Ciomas	Kadubeureum, Ciomas	PKI promoter. Collected money for the purchase of firearms. Proclaimed that those who were not members of the PKI would not be considered Moslems by the Sultan of Banten and would have their property confiscated. Arrested November 6, 1926.
36.	[Mohammed Nūr Fas] Nani	35	Tobacco stallkeeper	Kagunungan, Serang	Kagunungan, Serang	Arrested March 1, 1927.
37.	Tju Tong Hin	35	Trader	Pasar Baru, Batavia	Ciunjung, Rangkasbitung	PKI promoter among Chinese and local community in Rangkasbitung. Close confidant of Tjondrosaputro q.v. Arrested September 24, 1926.
38.	Sawiri	25	Peasant	Labuan, Anyer	Waringin, Anyer	PKI courier. Held meetings in the mosque after prayers. Arrested February 3, 1927.
39.	Ali Achmad	36	Peasant	Idem	Labuan, Anyer	PKI courier. Together with Sawiri (No. 38) close aide of Tje Mamat. Arrested March 4, 1927.
40.	Ali	45	Peasant	Sangiang, Anyer	Sangiang, Anyer	PKI courier. Arrested March 4, 1927.
41.	Tohir	20	Peasant	Labuan, Anyer	Labuan, Anyer	Arrested March 10, 1927.
42.	Djakaria	40	Peasant	Sigedang, Anyer	Idem	Arrested March 10, 1927.
43.	Samaden	50	Peasant	Sangiang, Anyer	Pasirbatang, Anyer	Arrested March 4, 1927.
44.	Moeslik	20	Peasant	Pabuaran, Ciomas	Pabuaran, Ciomas	PKI fundraiser; some peasants pawned their coconut patches to contribute monies to him. Arrested March 4, 1927.

Name	Age	Occupation	Place of Birth	Residence	Particulars
45. Mohammed Amin	45	Peasant	Sindangmandi, Ciomas	Sindangmandi, Ciomas	Former village clerk of Sindangmandi. Told local peasants that all whio worked for the government were to be killed, including his own brother who was the village headman. Arrested February 28, 1927.
46. H.Usman	50	Peasant	Silebu, Ciruas	Silebu, Ciruas	Influential PKI propagandist. Held meetings in langgar and mosques after evening prayers. Was appointed insurrectionary leader for the attack onWalantaka, then Ciruas and Serang.
47. Salikin	38	Religious teacher	Pancur, Serang	Pancur, Serang	Arrested September 1926 and sentenced to three months' imprisonment for the sale of amulets. Bathed many rebels in Serang area and afterwards dressed them in white. Also anointed others with holy oil to make them invulnerable.
48. Djari	42	Trader	Jalupang, Ciruas	Idem	
49. H. Asgari	26	Religious teacher	Gunungsari, Ciomas	Gunungsari, Ciomas	Urged his followers to revolt because of the burden of taxes.
50. Afif	27	Village clerk	Jombang, Cilegon	Labuan, Caringin	President PKI subsection Labuan. Commissaris PKI-DO. Went with Hasanuddin (q.v.) to purchase weapons in Batavia. Arrested September 8, 1926.
51. Hasanuddin	26	—	Maninjau, W. Sumatra	Jambatan Lima, Batavia	Replaced Puradisastra as Chairman of PKI Banten section. Went with Afif to buy arms in Batavia. Arrested 1926.

	Name	Age	Occupation	Place of Birth	Residence	Particulars
52	H. Emed	30	Religious teachers	Caringin	Caringin	Son of Kiyai Asnawi. Treasurer of PKI section Banten. Arrested November 17, 1926.
53.	Tb. H. Arifin	55	Peasant	Cikeusal, Pamarayan	Cikeusal, Pamarayan	Told the peasants of his village to gather on the night of November 12 for an attack on Serang.
54.	Tb. Moh. Isa	35	Peasant	Petir, Pamarayan	Petir, Pamarayan	One of the leaders of the attacks November 14 on the residence of the Assistant-Wedana of Petir.
55.	H. Jahja	42	Religious teacher/ trader	Idem	Idem	Idem
56.	Mohammed Isa	32	Trader	Sumurpecing, Serang	Sumurpecing, Serang	Arrested October 18, 1926.
57.	Tb. Mardjuk	36	Trader	Cikeusal, Pamarayan	Cikeusal, Pamarayan	Son of H. Arifin (No. 53). PKI propagandist. Arrested November 25, 1926.
58.	Mad Saleh	35	Peasant	Pabuaran, Ciomas	Pabuaran, Ciomas	PKI propagandist. Collected money which he told people would be used to hire a boat to convey arms from the Soviet Union. Arrested October 16, 1926, sentenced to ten months' imprisonment for assault.
59.	Abdullah	55	Peasant	Sumurpecing, Serang	Serang	Arrested October 18, 1926.
60.	Dulah	35	Bricklayer	Batavia	Idem	Arrested October 18, 1926.
61.	Alikasim	18	Peasant	Cirangkong, Pamarayan	Cirangkong, Pamarayan	—
62.	Mohammed Jusuf	25	Foreman, Public Works Department	Pabuaran, Ciomas	Kadubeureum, Ciomas	Arrested October 9, 1926.
63.	Mohammed Sis	48	Trader	Kaujon, Serang	Ciberang, Pandeglang	PKI courier. Arrested December 4, 1926.

	Name	Age	Occupation	Place of Birth	Residence	Particulars
64.	Surabaita	20	Trader	Keboncau, Pandeglang	Keboncau, Pandeglang	Influential PKI propagandist. On Pandeglang the night of November 12 gathered men in Kampung Pabrik for an attack on Pandeglang. Arrested December 4, 1926.
65.	Achmad Rifai	20	Clerk	Pandeglang	Sawah Besar, Batavia	Secretary PKI subsection Pandeglang. Arrested December 4, 1926.
66.	Mu'min	35	Peasant	Barugbug, Ciomas	Barugbug, Ciomas	PKI propagandist with much influence apparently because of his wealth and charisma. Said that all who did not contribute to PKI coffers would be robbed and killed. Arrested October 23, 1926.
67.	Umar	39	Peasant, ex-village head	Kaduagung, Ciomas	Kaduagung, Ciomas	Arrested October 23, 1926.
68.	H. Akjar	28	Peasant	Tejamari, Ciomas	Tejamari, Ciomas	Sentenced four times for breaking the ban on public meetings. Arrested November 12, 1926.
69.	Ishak	26	Typesetter, printing worker	Pandeglang	Serang	Chairman PKI subsection Serang. Arrested January 13, 1927.
70.	Tjondrosaputro	40	Trader	Central Java	Rangkasbitung	Chairman PKI subsection Rangkasbitung. Collected 200 guilders for arms purchases. Arrested late September 1926.
71.	Tb. Mohammed Hasjim alias Entjim	32	Agent, Singer Sewing-Machine Co.	Ciujung, Rangkasbitung	Ciujung, Rangkasbitung	Commissaris. PKI subsection Rangkasbitung. Arrested October 15,

	Name	Age	Occupation	Place of Birth	Residence	Particulars
72.	Kamim	35	Peasant	Pabuaran, Ciomas	Pabuaran, Ciomas	Arrested December 25, 1926.
73.	Salihun	35	Shoemaker	Cililitan, Batavia	Ciujung, Rangkasbitung	PKI propagandist and commissaris. Arrested September 24, 1926.
74.	Sera	35	Peasant	Malangkarsa, Ciruas	Malangkarsa, Ciruas	PKI propagandist sentenced to one year and nine months'imprisonment for robbery. Arrested October 19, 1926.
75.	H. Mardjuk	36	Peasant	Silebu, Ciruas	Kubang, Serang	Arrested February 5, 1927.
76.	H.Hasan	27	Peasant	Sajar, Serang	Pancur, Serang	PKI propagandist. Demanded one guilder from everybody he initiated into invulnerability rites. Arrested March 14, 1927.
77.	Ayot Satriawidjaja	26	Peasant	Kadugadung, Pandeglang	Kadugadung, Pandeglang	PKI courier. Arrested December 1, 1926.
78.	Mohammed Toha	23	Trader	Palanjar, Pandeglang	Palanjar, Pandeglang	Arrested December 11, 1926.
79.	Tb. Saleh	30	Peasant	Kudahandap, Pandeglang	Kudahandap, Pandeglang	Arrested December 10, 1926.
80.	K. H. Achmad	46	Religious teacher	Kaujon, Serang	Pancur, Serang	Religious teacher of great influence. Arrested April 20, 1927.
81.	Entol Enoh	40	Peasant, ex-village head	Nyamplong, Menes	Tegalwangi, Menes	Well known for his contacts with jawara. Leader of "semi-criminal" associations. Arrested December 4, 1926.
82.	Nawi	35	Peasant	Sukalaba, Ciomas	Sukalaba, Ciomas	Arrested November 6, 1926.
83.	Mohammed Arif	39	Peasant	Kapandean, Serang	Kapandean, Serang	Arrested October 23, 1926.
84.	Amir	32	Barber	Sumurpecung, Serang	Sumurpecung, Serang	Arrested October 18, 1926.

	Name	Age	Occupation	Place of Birth	Residence	Particulars
85.	Achmad Bassaif	23	—	Kaloran, Serang	Batavia	Arab father, Bantenese mother. Educated Al-Irsjad School, Batavia. Chairman PKI subsection Jembatan Lima, Batavia; chairman PKI subsection Tangerang; Acting Chairman PKI section Banten. Linkman between DO Banten and DO Batavia. Led attack on Glodok prison, Batavia. Arrested November 19, 1926. Sentenced eight years' imprisonment. Sent to Boven Digul, 1936.
86.	Mohammed Saleh	—	Policeman	Purworejo, Central Java	Serang	Arrested August 15, 1926.
87.	Atmodihardjo	—	Printing worker, journalist	Yogyakarta	Serang	PKI eommissaris. Organizer of strike on *De Ban ten Bode*. Arrested August 15, 1926.
88.	Asmail	32	Peasant	Pabuaran,	Kadubeureum,	Arrested October 7, 1926.
89.	H. Mohammed Salim	30	Penghulu (religious official)	Babakanlor, Caringin	Babakanlor, Caringin	Recruited into the PKI by Haji Achmad Chatib. Key leader of the revolt in Menes. Detained by the police in Serang for questioning on November 11, but released in time to catch the last train home to participate in the revolt. Arrested January 14, 1927.
90.	Karis	29	Peasant	Rancapare, Serang	Rancapare, Serang	Arrested October 22, 1926.
91.	Aliakbar	36	Laborer	Passar, Serang	Passar, Serang	Arrested October 22, 1926.
92.	Rujani	28	Tailor	Rancapare, Serang	Kagunungan, Serang	Arrested March 3, 1927.

Name	Age	Occupation	Place of Birth	Residence	Particulars
93. H. Aliasgar	36	Peasant	Pancangan, Serang	Silebu, Ciruas	Arrested February 5, 1927.
94. Entjang	32	Peasant	Cilanggawe, Caringin	Cilanggawe, Caringin	Arrested March 10, 1927.
95. Mohammed	35	Peasant	Karunang, Ciomas	Karunang, Ciomas	Arrested November 6, 1926.
96. Abdulkarim	30	Peasant	Pancur, Serang	Ciliwong, Serang	Arrested April 20, 1927.
97. H. Achmed	40	Peasant	Rancapare, Serang	Rancapare, Serang	Arrested March 10, 1927.
98. Andung	35	Peasant	Pabuaran, Ciomas	Pabuaran, Ciomas	Arrested October 22, 1926.
99. Hardjosuparto	22	Trader	Rangkasbitung	Rangkasbitung	Arrested October 22, 1926.

Abbreviations: K. Kiyai

H. = Haji

Tb. = Tubagas (male descendant of Sultans of Banten).

Sources: Vb March 4, 1927; Report of Resident of Banten, August 29, 1927 in Mailr 523x/1927; Mailr 1966x/1927; Report of Resident of Banten, December 23, 1927 in Mailr 1074x/28; Mailr 113x/1928; Mailr 637x/1928.

Interviews with the following ex-Digulists: Afif (No. 50), Achmad Rifai (No. 65), Ayot Satriawidjaja (No. 77), Achmad Bassaif (No. 85).

APPENDIX TWO
BANTENESE SENTENCED TO LIFE IMPRISONMENT

Name	Place of Residence	Occupation
Salija	Bonjongjanar, Menes	Peasant
Kadiman	Idem	Idem
Marsani	Bangko, Labuan	Idem
Idris	Kalumpang, Labuan	Idem
H. Hasan	Tarogog, Labuan	Idem
Saleh	Jiput, Labuan	Idem
Salman	Idem	Idem
Rasiman	Idem	Idem
Djasiin	Pagelaran, Labuan	Idem

APPENDIX THREE
LIST OF BANTENESE EXECUTED

	Name	Place of Residence	Occupation
1.	Jas'a	Kenega, Menes	Peasant
2.	Jamin	Idem	Idem
3.	Doelsalam	Tegalwangi, Menes	Idem
4.	H. Asikin	Cipucung, Menes	Idem

CPSIA information can be obtained at www.ICGtesting.com
Printed in the USA
BVOW021105200612

293197BV00002B/60/P